THE CORNERSTONE BLUEPRINT

STEVEN J. ADDARIO, JR.

ISBN: 979-8-9946300-1-3

Published by The Ghost Publishing, LLC

CONTENTS

"First we build our habits, then our habits build us."

For Alison, Steven, Bella, Ayla, and Dante —
my heart, my courage, my joy.

To my whole family, especially my parents, Big Steve and
Betty, who have been my anchor in every storm and my
inspiration in every triumph.

You are the reason I dream bigger and push harder.
You are the reason I chose legacy over comfort.
This book was written with you in mind, and for the
generations that will follow us.

May these words be a reminder that our foundation is strong,
our love is unshakable,
and our purpose is eternal.

ACKNOWLEDGMENTS

No book is ever the product of one person alone. Though my name may be on the cover, this work is the fruit of countless influences, sacrifices, conversations, and encouragements that have shaped me over the years. It is only right to pause here, at the close of these pages, and honor those whose presence has made this book possible.

First and foremost, I thank my family. To my wife, Alison—my high school sweetheart, partner, and confidante, your love and faith in me have been the steady light that kept me grounded through every season. You have borne the weight of my ambitions with grace and patience. There were times when the late nights, the long days, and the endless striving could have left us divided, but instead, you chose to stand with me. Your belief has fueled mine, and this book would never have come to life without you.

To my children, Steven, Bella, Ayla, and Dante, and each of you who call me Dad and Uncle, you are the heartbeat of everything I do. Every page of this book, every idea, every strategy has been tested against the question: 'Will this make life better for you, and for those who come after you?' I write not only to the world, but to you. May these words remind you that anything is possible when you stand on a strong foundation. You are my greatest teachers and my greatest legacy.

I owe deep gratitude to the teachers and mentors who shaped my journey. To Dr. John DeMartini, your teachings on values, fulfillment, and the seven areas of life opened my mind to the possibility of living a fully integrated life. Your Breakthrough Experience gave me tools that are woven into every chapter here. To Dr. Matt James and Dr John Ryan, your mastery of NLP and the 4MAT system helped me not only learn but teach in a way that transforms. Your influence guided the very framework of this book.

To Sean Webb, thank you for your work on emotional algorithms and the Webb Framework. Your insights gave language to the inner mechanics of the human heart and mind. To Chad Wright, your Navy SEAL principles of patience, presence, and deliberateness taught me the value of grit and grace combined. My deepest gratitude goes to my Karate instructor, Jason Scaduto, who has walked beside me in training for more than fifteen years. Under his teaching, I earned my second-degree black belt, but more importantly, I gained the discipline, resilience, and honor that will serve me for a lifetime. His legacy lives on in every student he has shaped, including me.

To my team at Addario's Services, you are the hands and feet of the vision. Every day, you show up not just to do a job, but to serve people and solve problems that matter. The lessons I've learned leading alongside you are etched into the practices I share in these pages. Thank you for your trust and commitment, for believing in a vision bigger than any one of us.

To the Trades Talk community, business owners, leaders, and dreamers, you are the reason this book exists. Your hunger to grow, to lead, to break through limitations has inspired me time and again. Our conversations, our events, and our shared struggles gave shape to the stories, principles, and strategies within these chapters. You reminded me that leadership is not about perfection but about courage. Thank you for allowing me to walk with you on your journey.

I also want to thank Mike A., Rob Z., and Mike D. Each of you pushed me to go further than I thought I could go. You believed in me when my own belief wavered. You challenged me, stretched me, and demanded more of me until I discovered the strength and vision that had been there all along. Without your influence, I may never have uncovered the true depth of what was inside me.

To my friends who stood beside me, often without recognition, thank you for the quiet words of encouragement, the challenging questions, and the honest conversations that sharpened me. Iron sharpens iron, and I am stronger because of you.

Finally, to you the reader. Thank you for picking up this book and trusting me to speak into your life. Time is the most precious resource, and you chose to spend yours here. My hope is that these words serve not as theories but as tools, practical, usable, and transformative. If something in these pages helped you see yourself, your family, your vocation, or your legacy differently, then this work has done its job. You are the living continuation of these ideas. Your application is the true acknowledgment.

No one builds alone. No one grows alone. And no one leaves a legacy alone. This book stands as a testament to the fact that we rise together. As I close these words, I do so with humility and gratitude. May the acknowledgments you have just read not be the end of thanks, but the beginning of a chain of gratitude that flows forward, into your life, your family, your business, and the generations to come.

PREFACE

Every book has a story behind it, but this one has a heartbeat. It comes from decades of building, falling, getting back up, and realizing that no matter how much money you make, no matter how many wins you stack, if the foundation of life isn't right, the entire structure wobbles and ultimately falls.

In my journey through business, family, and personal growth, I discovered that achievement in one area doesn't always translate into fulfillment across all areas. I've had times when the business thrived, but my health suffered, or when finances were booming, but relationships were strained. Those moments taught me an undeniable truth: success without balance is failure in disguise.

The Cornerstone Blueprint emerged out of this tension. I needed a framework that wasn't just about making money, personal development, or leadership. I needed something that wove all areas of life together, something holistic, something timeless, something that worked.

This book is written for those who feel the same pull. It's for the achievers who are tired of burning out. It's for the dreamers who want more than dreams; who want their reality to reflect their wildest dreams. It's for leaders, parents, builders, and visionaries who sense that their life is meant to be lived at a higher level of integration.

What you hold in your hands is not a theory. Theories, at best, are educated guesses, interpretations built on assumptions, and observations that pass off as probabilities. Theories invite discussion; blueprints, on the other hand, provide clear, precise instructions. You're holding a blueprint, my friend. It's not a collection of motivational slogans; it's a system. You'll see that it's practical, but it's also deeply personal. Each chapter is built with space for reflection and application, because transformation doesn't happen by reading, it happens by applying what you've learned. That's when the really good living starts.

My promise is simple: if you engage with this book honestly and put these cornerstones and pillars into practice, you will not only achieve more but also live a better, more fulfilled life. And in the end, that's what matters.

This is not the end of my journey; it's a waypoint. Volume 1 focuses on life. Volume 2 will focus on business. Together, they will give you a system for mastery in both. But for now, let's start where it all begins, with life itself.

INTRODUCTION –
THE SPRINGBOARD

We are living in an age of noise. Every device in your pocket, every screen on your wall, every voice online tells you what to want, how to think, and who to be. Yet amid this constant noise, people are more anxious, more disconnected, and more uncertain than ever before.

I learned this lesson the hard way. Early in my career, I thought if I just worked hard enough, built enough, and achieved enough, I would finally feel whole. I checked the boxes—money, recognition, growth, but found myself restless, wondering, 'Is this it?' The truth hit me: building on shaky foundations guarantees collapse. One storm, whether financial, relational, or personal, can crumble everything you thought was secure.

That realization forced me to ask more profound questions. What is life really built on? What holds up when storms hit? The answers didn't come overnight, but through years of searching, leading, failing, and trying again. What emerged was a framework that could be trusted. I call it the Four Cornerstones: Belief, Knowledge, Consistency, and Results.

These Four Cornerstones form the unshakable foundation of everything you build. But foundations alone don't make a house. They are meant to support something bigger. That's where the Seven Pillars of Life come in, spiritual, mental, vocational, financial, familial, social, and physical. Together, they give structure to a whole life.

This book, Volume 1, is about life. How do you build a life that's not just successful, but whole? How do you integrate belief, knowledge, consistency, and results into every area so that nothing is left behind? That is the journey we're about to take.

Each chapter blends teaching with reflection. You'll find truths, questions, and space to insert your own stories. You'll see my lessons, the wins, the failures, the pivots, but the most important part will be your story. Because the Cornerstone Blueprint is not about me, it's about you.

This introduction is the springboard. Ahead, we will dive into the foundation: the Four Cornerstones. Master these, and you'll have the strength to build in any storm. Then we'll move into the Seven Pillars, the areas that make life rich, balanced, and complete.

Take a deep breath. Clear the noise. Open your heart and your mind. The blueprint begins now.

PART ONE
THE FOUNDATION: THE FOUR CORNERSTONES

"The foundation of every great life is built, not found."

— ANONYMOUS

The journey begins at the ground level — the bedrock that everything else must rest upon. The Four Cornerstones are not abstract ideas, but living principles: Belief, Knowledge, Consistency, and Results. This first section is about laying the base that will support every decision, every challenge, and every victory you face. Before we climb into the seven areas of life, we must ensure your foundation is solid. When these stones are set in place, nothing can shake the structure of your life.

We begin with Belief, because before you can build anything outside, you must first build inside.

CHAPTER ONE
BELIEF: THE LENS THAT SHAPES YOUR LIFE

---

*"Whether you think you can, or you think you can't—
you're right."*

— HENRY FORD

BELIEF

EVERYONE STARTS FORMING BELIEFS BEFORE THEY CAN think or express emotion (other than crying or cooing). Belief is the first builder of your life. We were not told to believe we can walk. We saw our parents and others walking, and, innately, deep down in our baby-subconscious, we believed we could walk. Most of us fell a few times, but without being able to reason it out, we knew we were meant to walk, and look at us now!

Now, as an adult, before any decision, before any action, before any result, there is a belief. However, this belief isn't as innate as walking; it comes from a mixture of our upbringing - authority figures such as parents, older siblings, teachers, etc., the music or television shows that played in your house as a child, and by witnessing violence, love, peace, or a religion, if your parents held true to their warnings and you got spanked, put on timeout, or got off Scott-free. Our early years' experiences shaped the beliefs we hold to be true today.

Beliefs act as the lens of a camera: they don't change reality itself, but they absolutely determine how reality is framed. Two people can face the same obstacle; one sees opportunity, the other sees doom. The difference? The lens of belief. The question is not whether you have beliefs; the question is whether your beliefs are serving you or sabotaging you.

Picture two entrepreneurs. Both are given the same resources, the same training, and even the same script for their business. One takes off, builds wealth, and inspires others. The other struggles, hesitates, and eventually quits. What created the gap? It wasn't knowledge or opportunity. It was belief. One believed, 'I can learn anything and figure this out.' The other believed, 'I'm not cut out for this.' 'There's too much established competition.' Or whatever reason they allow themselves to believe to quit. That single difference in belief shaped every action and, ultimately, every result.

Belief is powerful because it is often invisible. You don't wake up saying, "Today, I will live out my beliefs." You simply live. You speak, you act, you choose, and beneath it all, beliefs are whispering instructions and pulling invisible levers that show real-world results. Some beliefs empower. Others sabotage.

The problem most people need to realize about their beliefs is this: your beliefs are not facts, and they're not etched in stone forever. They are thoughts you chose, or that were ingrained in you. Those thoughts manifest into decisions, decisions you can question, replace, and rewire. The moment you realize that beliefs are chosen lenses, not unchangeable truths, is the moment you step into personal freedom.

One of the things I wish more people knew what that they don't truly know what *their* beliefs are! They settled on their Life-Script when they were 12 or 13-years-old, and never challenged them, never questioned them, never sought supporting data to support it. This is why so many people feel lost today– they have never truly found themselves. One of my hopes for this book is that it motivates to challenge everything you thought you could and could not do.

THE FOUR CORNERSTONES

Imagine your life as a house. The Four Cornerstones: Belief, Knowledge, Consistency, and Results, are the foundation stones. If belief is cracked, the entire foundation trembles. No matter how much knowledge you gather, how hard you work, or how many results you chase, if deep down you believe you are unworthy, broken, or incapable, your structure will eventually collapse.

Belief is the ignition key of life. You can have a Lamborghini parked in the garage – the Lambo is a metaphor for knowledge, resources, networks, and opportunities, but without the ignition key of belief, the engine never roars to life. How many people have all the tools and yet stall at the start line because their key of belief is missing? Have you ever seen a bad sales rep fix and fidget around with his desk and chair, and go to the bathroom and talk to everyone instead of picking up the phone and making money for the company and his family? It's not that he's outgoing – he doesn't believe he can make sales!

Belief is the compass of your life. It quietly sets your direction. If your compass is calibrated toward possibility, you move boldly, even through storms. If it is set toward fear, every road looks dangerous, and you hesitate, even when the path is safe.

Belief is the soil of your life. Your talents, opportunities, and relationships are seeds. Plant them in rocky, barren soil and they wither. Plant them in rich, healthy soil, and they multiply. Upgrade the soil, and every seed you touch grows stronger.

Belief is the thermostat of your life. If it's set low, no matter how much success you achieve, you unconsciously sabotage until you return to what feels familiar.

Raise your belief thermostat and the climate of your life rises with it. Think about people who win the lottery only to be broke within five years—they didn't raise their belief thermostat around wealth. On the other hand, someone who upgrades their belief thermostat can turn even modest opportunities into extraordinary results.

Imagine living one week under the belief, 'I am not enough.' On Monday, you hold back from speaking in a meeting – no one even remembers you were there. On Tuesday, you avoid eye contact with someone you admire – and the next person that says hi to him ends up having lunch with him. By Wednesday, you turn down an opportunity because you feel unqualified – and you go home believing there's a shortage of opportunities in your company. By Friday, the week has passed in quiet resignation. The belief has silently written the script of your life.

Now imagine the same week lived under the belief, 'I am resourceful and capable.' On Monday, you raise your hand with confidence – you make a great point and your supervisor wants to meet with you to further explain. On Tuesday, you smile and connect with someone new – you find out you both love the same team, end up going to a game together, and become good friends. By Wednesday, you say yes to a stretch opportunity and figure it out as you go – since you're the guy with the great idea on Monday, they give you the opportunity and room to figure it out. By Friday, you feel a sense of momentum and pride. The external circumstances haven't changed, your belief has. And with it, the story of your week, which repeats over and over and becomes the story of your life.

WHY DOESN'T DAD LOVE ME?

I can still picture it like yesterday. The street was quiet in the early morning; the kind of silence that only exists before the world wakes up. My dad's voice broke the stillness: *"It's time to catch bad guys."*

I was six years old, eyes heavy, body still begging for sleep because it was 4 AM. It was time for my sister to deliver the Boston Globe newspapers. However, as her younger brother, but the eldest boy in the house, my father assigned me to be her helper. (I would do this for five years without pay, until my sister 'retired' and then I did them by myself.)

The stack of newspapers looked like a mountain to me. Monday through Saturday, we had to deliver 100 papers; on Sundays, 200. The cold air stung my face as the Bronco drove up and down the streets, with me hanging on to the back of the car, jumping off, delivering the paper, and jumping back on at each stop. (This would be considered highly illegal today, but those were different times!)

I wasn't the only kid with a paper route, but I was certainly the one with the longest one. Over the years, a thought continually circled in my head, particularly when dealing with the ice-cold winter months in Massachusetts: *Why me? Why would my dad do this to me if he loved me?*

That belief took root. I convinced myself that maybe my dad didn't really like me. That maybe I wasn't the son he wanted. The words he never said filled the silence louder than anything he could have spoken. And every early morning, sitting on that tailgate, the belief grew stronger.

That belief shaped my actions. I pushed harder, not out of joy, but out of a need to prove something, maybe to him, maybe to myself. I envied my friends who got to sleep in, who had fathers who seemed softer. Doubt crept in every step of the route. My "job" not only limited my sleep, but also my social life. I couldn't sleep over my friends' houses because I had to be up early every morning. When my father was questioned why I couldn't sleep over my friend's house one time, he said, very matter-of-factly:v"Well, I don't want to go over and wake you all up at four in the morning to bring Steven to work." My mind was made up. He hated me. At best, he really didn't like me.

Psychologists describe the self-fulfilling prophecy, but long before science gave it a label, humanity knew the pattern: what you believe shapes what you notice, which shapes what you choose, which shapes what you create. In Neuro Linguistic Programming (NLP), this is captured in the belief-behavior-result loop: Belief → Behavior → Result → Reinforced Belief. This loop becomes a cycle of destiny. Unless interrupted, it will keep spinning endlessly.

If you believe 'I'm terrible at relationships,' you stop trying, your behavior communicates insecurity, your relationships struggle, and the result reinforces the belief. The loop tightens. But if you believe, 'I am capable of learning love,' you show up with curiosity, your behavior shifts, relationships improve, and the result strengthens the new belief. The loop becomes virtuous instead of vicious.

History is filled with stories of belief shaping destiny. Thomas Edison famously said, 'I have not failed. I've just found 10,000 ways that won't work.' If he had believed failure defined him, the light bulb would not exist. Nelson Mandela spent 27 years in prison. If he had believed he was powerless, South Africa would not have seen the birth of a new democracy. Belief doesn't erase obstacles; it transforms them into steppingstones.

In athletics, the 'four-minute mile' was once considered impossible. Doctors claimed the human body would collapse if pushed that far. But when Roger Bannister broke it in 1954, everything changed. Within a year, multiple athletes also broke the barrier. The difference wasn't in physiology; it was in belief. Once the mental ceiling was shattered, the body followed.

Consider Michael Jordan. Cut from his high school basketball team, he could have believed, 'I'm not good enough.' Instead, he chose to believe, 'I will work harder than anyone else.' That belief fueled his practice, sharpened his skills, and carried him into history as one of the greatest players of all time.

Or take Bruce Lee Told he was too small, too foreign, and too broken-English to matter, Bruce believed differently. He saw himself as a bridge between cultures, between philosophy and martial arts, between body and spirit. His belief in personal freedom created a martial and cultural revolution.

Here's a step-by-step walkthrough for reshaping beliefs using NLP

1. Identify a limiting belief ('I don't deserve success').
2. Notice its sensory qualities—where do you feel it? What does it look like in your mind? What voice repeats it?
3. Alter its sub modalities: make the image small and far away, lower the volume of the voice, lighten the feeling.
4. Bring up a powerful memory when you felt unstoppable. Amplify it—brighten the image, turn up the sound, breathe into the feeling.
5. Anchor this by pressing your fingers together or making a gesture.
6. State the empowering belief: 'I deserve success, and I claim it.' Repeat it while anchored.
7. Future pace: see yourself walking into tomorrow's challenges with this belief alive inside you.

Repeat daily until the new belief feels natural and automatic.

Imagine waking up tomorrow with the belief, 'I am unstoppable.' You rise from bed with energy. You approach challenges as games to play, not threats to fear. Conversations flow easily because you believe you belong. Opportunities seem to find you because your energy broadcasts confidence. By the end of the day, you've taken bold steps you might once have avoided. The belief didn't just change your mood, it changed your trajectory.

What if you believed rejection wasn't personal, but redirection? Suddenly, every 'no' would point you toward a better 'yes.' What if you believed failure wasn't final, but feedback? You'd experiment more, learn faster, and grow stronger.

What if you believed wealth wasn't reserved for a chosen few, but available to anyone who created value? Your creativity would unlock, your work ethic would intensify, and opportunities would expand. Belief is the invisible hand that pushes you forward or holds you back.

As a kid, I couldn't understand why my father, or any father who supposedly loved his son, would drag a six-year-old out of bed before dawn to deliver 100 newspapers every morning, 200 on Sundays. My hands would sting from the cold as I wrestled with stacks of papers taller than me. Friends were sleeping over at each other's houses, but not me. I had to be home. The route was waiting.

At that age, I didn't have the perspective to see it as discipline. What I felt was frustration and confusion. The story I told myself was simple: My dad doesn't like me. Maybe he doesn't even love me. That belief hardened with each dark morning I stumbled half-asleep through the neighborhood, doing work that none of my friends had to do.

By the time I was old enough to get "real working papers," I ran to a normal after-school job, adding shifts after football practice and carrying that grind straight through high school. There was never a break, never a season of ease. I graduated, went right into my trade, and by 21 I was already building my own business. On the outside, I looked driven. On the inside, I was still fueled by that old thermostat setting: prove yourself, because your father never really liked you.

EVERYONE IS DOING THE BEST THEY CAN WITH WHAT THEY HAVE

Then one day, in my twenties, I was sitting in a seminar, half-distracted, when I heard a trainer say something that cracked my old belief wide open:

"Everyone is doing the best they can with what they have."

When I understood the meaning of that sentence, it hit me harder than any cold-morning winter blast or football drill ever did. For the first time, I stopped judging my dad by what I thought love was supposed to look like. I saw him as a man, not just as my father. A man who didn't have the emotionally expressive language of affection. A man who believed that the best way to prepare his son for life was to harden him early, to teach him grit through repetition, to make responsibility second nature.

My long-held belief was being challenged. So, he wasn't cruel? He was preparing me the best way he knew how?

In that moment, my belief thermostat upgraded. The old story, my dad doesn't like me, collapsed. With new data, a new story took root: my dad LOVED me so much and was shaping me into the man, leader, and father I am today. What once felt like rejection became my foundation. He didn't always have the words, but he had the intention. And his intention was to prepare me, even if he had to demand from me, in order to forge me like a well-made sword.

That new belief didn't just change how I saw my past, it changed how I lived my present. I stopped running from the grind. I stopped resenting responsibility. Instead, I embraced them as gifts, as training, as proof that I could handle more than most people were willing to shoulder.

Looking back now, I see it all differently. Those paper routes, those long days of school, football, and work, they weren't punishments. They were foundations. They built the discipline that allowed me to launch my own company at 21. They shaped the resilience I needed to lead a family of my own. They gave me the internal thermostat to handle stress, setbacks, and responsibility without crumbling.

What once felt like proof that my father didn't like me has become proof that he loved me in the only way he knew how, by preparing me for the weight of life.

"Everyone is doing the best they can with what they have." That one belief turned resentment into gratitude, and burden into foundation."

THE BELIEF THERMOSTAT

THE CONTRACT

Beliefs are like contracts. Many of us are living under agreements we didn't consciously sign, agreements inherited from parents, culture, or past pain. The good news is, you can tear up the old contracts and write new ones. You can choose agreements that serve your future, not bind you to your past.

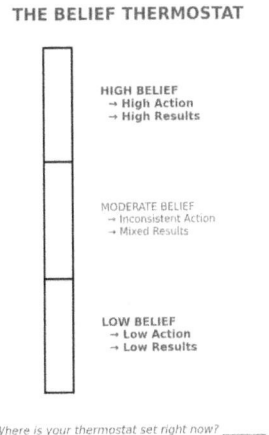

HIGH BELIEF
→ High Action
→ High Results

MODERATE BELIEF
→ Inconsistent Action
→ Mixed Results

LOW BELIEF
→ Low Action
→ Low Results

Where is your thermostat set right now? _____

CORNERSTONE TRUTHS

1. Beliefs are decisions, not facts.
2. Your results mirror your beliefs.
3. New beliefs can be installed through awareness, evidence, and repetition.

REFLECTION QUESTIONS

1. What belief is currently limiting your life?
2. What has it cost you in relationships, health, or wealth?
3. What new belief would change everything if you lived it?

"When you change what you believe, you change what you receive."

CHAPTER TWO

KNOWLEDGE: THE MAP OF MASTERY

"An investment in knowledge pays the best interest."

— BENJAMIN FRANKLIN

KNOWLEDGE

BELIEF GIVES YOU THE CONFIDENCE TO BEGIN, KNOWLEDGE shows you where to go. Knowledge is the map of mastery. Without it, you stumble in the dark, making the same mistakes over and over again. With it, you gain sight, strategy, and shortcuts. Belief is the ignition key, but knowledge is the GPS. You can believe in yourself all day long, but if you don't know the road, you'll circle endlessly.

Think of explorers setting out centuries ago. Those with accurate maps could cross oceans, discover new lands, and return with treasures. Those without maps drifted aimlessly, ran out of supplies, and often never returned. Knowledge was not just power, it was survival. Even today, the same principle applies. In business, in relationships, in health, those who have maps navigate. Those who don't, wander.

Why pursue knowledge? Because ignorance is expensive. Mistakes repeated out of ignorance cost time, money, energy, or relationships. Why not pursue knowledge? Because it demands humility. It requires admitting you don't know, asking questions, seeking mentors, and enduring discomfort. For many, ego becomes the barrier. They would rather look smart than become wise.

Knowledge is like a compass and map combined. Belief may get you moving, but without a map, you may run enthusiastically in the wrong direction. Every step feels productive, but at the end of the journey, you arrive at the wrong destination. Imagine climbing a tall ladder with relentless effort, only to realize it was leaning against the wrong wall. That is the cost of ignorance.

Unfortunately, many driven, ambitious, and highly motivated people let their pride shield them from success. They're intelligent, hands-on people who have it in them to do much better, but their I-can-do-it-on-my-own attitude makes them go the long way around. Others turn to the wrong mentors. They get advice from people who are in their same situation or worse! They're handed a map that's based on theory, not experience. It's like following a GPS to your mother's house but you're trying to go to church.

But let me tell you an interesting thing about following the right map that perhaps you've never heard – no one has a forever map! Business owners who continue to grow personally as well as their businesses understand that they need to follow the correct Right Now map. If you're making $200K a year, don't follow the Billionaire map just yet. Follow the $500K map. Once you reach $500K, switch to the million-dollar map, then to the $5 million map. If you continue to upgrade yourself and your business, you'll eventually be ready to understand the billionaire map. You may have a good map but if you're not ready, it's not your Right Now map.

MODELING

In NLP, one of the most powerful principles is modeling. Modeling means studying the strategies, beliefs, and patterns of someone who has already achieved what you desire. Knowledge is not just information—it is organized insight. When you model excellence, you borrow decades of trial and error and compress it into days. This is why apprenticeships worked for centuries —learners absorbed not just facts, but frameworks, instincts, and ways of seeing the world.

Consider Warren Buffett, one of the greatest investors in history. His success is built on compounding knowledge. Buffett doesn't rest on his resume, he doesn't rest on his laurels, and he doesn't rest on past accomplishments; he still reads for hours every single day. He doesn't do it for entertainment—he does it as an investment in himself. He knows that as his knowledge increases, so do his educated guesses, and as the knowledge sinks into his subconscious, it sharpens his instincts. Each page refines his map of the financial world. His belief in himself as an investor didn't come easy or by luck; it was the outcome of relentless learning. Without knowledge, his belief would have been arrogance.

Or look at Tom Brady. A very good but not great college career brought him into the NFL as a sixth-round draft pick whom few expected to succeed, but knowledge turned him into the greatest quarterback of all time. Even though he wasn't a starter, which meant he didn't play in the games, he still devoured playbooks and studied defenses until he could anticipate their moves. He was as prepared as he could possibly be when he finally had a chance to play. He quickly applied his knowledge to real-game experiences and started winning. But then, he needed a new map – he was getting older, and, because the NFL drafts players every year, his competition was getting younger. He found a new Right Now map and obsessed over nutrition, biomechanics, and recovery.

Brady didn't just rely on raw talent—he built a mental library that gave him an edge over faster, stronger opponents. Every film session became a classroom, every mistake a lesson. Knowledge wasn't just information to him; it was fuel for mastery.

Steve Jobs famously combined knowledge of design, technology, and human psychology. The iPhone wasn't just technology; it was an elegant map of how humans wanted to connect. Jobs knew what people wanted even though they didn't yet. That level of knowledge requires curiosity, relentless learning, and synthesis.

When I first started my business, I was winging it every single day. No formal business training. No blueprint. Just grit, hustle, and a willingness to outwork anyone, thanks to my father. And to be fair, that hustle paid off. In the first 16 months, I grew the business to over a million dollars in revenue. On paper, it looked like I had cracked the code.

But underneath the numbers, there was chaos. I didn't have pricing models—I had guesses. I didn't have scripts for answering phones—whoever was near it when it rang picked it up, and I had no idea what they would say. Dispatching jobs? It was more juggling than a system; I'm surprised my drivers got to where they needed to be sometimes. While hustle got me far, I lacked structure. And that lack of structure cost me something monumental: sustainability.

Deep down, I knew it. I knew sheer effort could only carry me so far before it broke me or broke the business. What I knew had brought me to where I was, I had to find out what I didn't know.

Somewhere between 2003 and 2005, I stumbled into a seminar hosted by a best practices group. It felt like stepping behind the curtain of Oz. These guys had it all mapped out—the phone scripts, the dispatch systems, the pricing formulas, the training structures. Everything I had been winging, they had already engineered.

I remember sitting there in shock, realizing that what had taken me blood and sweat just to hold together was already available, tested, proven, and packaged. Knowledge wasn't just power. Knowledge was leverage.

But here's the truth: I didn't act. I left that seminar fired up, but went back to winging it. For nearly two years, I pushed forward the only way I knew how, muscle and hustle, while systems sat there waiting to be adopted. That delay cost me millions.

In 2006, I finally drew the line. I joined that best practices group. This time I didn't just listen, I acted. We rolled up our sleeves and began implementing systems and processes piece by piece. Pricing was no longer random, it made sense to the customers and to us. Phones were answered with intention. We stopped missing out on leads and opportunities because we knew which questions to ask and how to answer their questions. Dispatch became predictable. Our guys got to where they needed to be on time, with minimal chaos, and prepared to do the job at hand.

I want to challenge something you may have heard - knowledge is power. It's not. You can know how to make your grandmother's famous stew, but if you never cook it, you won't feed anyone. What I'm saying is that knowledge gets you close to power, it turns into power when it's applied. When I first heard how I could improve my business, nothing changed because I didn't apply it. Once I did, the business shifted. We had clarity where there used to be confusion. We had systems where there used to be chaos.

I have a quick question for you, dear reader – if you've already learned something in this book, what are you going to do with that new knowledge?

And then came the realization that changed everything again: even the best systems and processes have one wildcard, the people who run them. Knowledge gave me the blueprint, but leadership gave me the leverage.

That season taught me a lesson I'll never forget: hustle builds momentum, but knowledge builds empires. Without the systems I learned and implemented, my company would have stayed a house of cards. With them, it became something sustainable.

Looking back, I see the cost of delaying action. But I also see the power of finally leaning into knowledge. It shifted my entire thermostat. I no longer saw learning as optional. The problem for the 87% of businesses that don't make it five years is that the leader may know exactly how to do the job, but they never increase their knowledge of how to expand the business, trim the fat, or be more consistent. For me, that applied knowledge became my competitive advantage. Every new strategy, every coaching session, every leadership framework wasn't just information—it was compound interest on the future of my business.

"Hustle builds momentum. Knowledge builds empires."

Knowledge builds in stages.

- Unconscious Incompetence – you don't know what you don't know.
- Conscious Competence – you become aware of your gaps.
- Conscious Competence – you practice deliberately – repetition, repetition, repetition.

Finally, repetition leads to unconscious competence—mastery that feels automatic. Most people quit in stage two because awareness of ignorance feels uncomfortable. Masters push through discomfort until skill becomes second nature.

What if you treated knowledge as your greatest asset? Imagine giving as much energy to learning as most people give to entertainment. Instead of scrolling endlessly on your phone, you invested those hours in studying. Instead of chasing gossip, you sought wisdom. Your relationships would deepen because you better understood human behavior. Your finances would grow because instead of working for money, you would know how to make money work for you. Your health would improve because you understood how the body works.

What if you believed one of the biggest truths in life - ignorance is too expensive to afford? What if you looked at books as an investment of your money and time? What if you saw each seminar as a shortcut? What if you saw a mentor as a cheat code and each coach as having a competitive advantage? The gap between where you are and where you want to be shrinks with every new insight you apply.

Knowledge creates new maps in your mind. NLP teaches that 'the map is not the territory.' Your inner map of reality determines how you navigate life. Expand your map through knowledge, and new possibilities appear. If your map of money only says, 'work harder,' you'll miss opportunities for leverage. If your map of relationships says, 'love always ends in pain,' you'll miss intimacy. Update the map, and you update your life.

Practical knowledge doesn't just stay in your head; it changes how you live. Knowledge of nutrition changes your meals. Knowledge of persuasion changes your conversations. Knowledge of spirituality changes your peace. Wisdom is applied knowledge, and applied knowledge builds legacy.

By 2015, my business had systems. Pricing wasn't random. Phones were answered with intention. Dispatch worked. The business no longer felt like a house of cards. Yet something still nagged at me: even the best systems have one wildcard, the people who run them.

I began to see it everywhere. Processes worked on paper but failed in practice because of the human factor. Employees got stuck in old patterns. Leaders burned out. Talent plateaued. I could install the finest systems in the world, but if I didn't understand *the operators*, the systems would eventually break.

Then, by pure accident, I attended my first NLP seminar. At the time, I didn't even know exactly what NLP was. I only knew I was desperate to understand how people operate, their mental "code," their operating systems, and whether that code could be changed.

Walking into that seminar was like stepping through a door I didn't know existed. Over the next several days, I realized I'd been trying to drive high-performance cars without ever learning to work on the engine. NLP gave me a diagnostic kit for human behavior.

That event sent me on a three-year journey. I didn't dabble. I immersed myself. Seminars, trainings, coaching, practice. Learning how beliefs are formed and how they can be rewritten. How language patterns shape decisions. How state, focus, and self-talk can be shifted in real time.

I felt like I'd been unplugged from the matrix. For the first time, I understood not just what people were doing but *why*. I could see the hidden scripts. I could help my team get unstuck. I could coach people toward the success they wanted but didn't yet have the skills to reach.

This wasn't just more "business knowledge." This was human operating-system knowledge. And it changed everything. It made me a better leader, a better coach, a better father, and a better friend.

"Systems run on processes. Results run on people. Mastering the human operating system is the ultimate leverage."

Imagine two people facing the same problem. One relies only on belief and grit, swinging powerfully but blindly. The other has studied, sought mentors, and carries his Right Now map. Whose reputation grows faster? Who gets more referrals? Who can start charging more? One struggles for years, the other finds solutions in months. Applied knowledge is the difference between decades of wandering and a focused path to mastery.

Imagine waking up tomorrow with the belief, 'Every day I grow wiser.' You'd approach conversations with curiosity rather than judgement. You'd ask questions and get answers to things you've been struggling with for years. You'd leave conversations enlightened with new thoughts, ideas, and excitement.

Books would feel like the treasure maps they are. A poor person once complained to a rich person, "Why don't you rich people give your secrets to us poor people?"

The rich person, who was born poor but made himself rich, answered, "But they did leave their secrets, they're just hidden."

"Hidden where?"

The rich man's eyes gleamed, "In books!"

Mentors would feel like expert guides. Over weeks and months, your knowledge would compound into confidence, and confidence into mastery.

THE KNOWLEDGE PYRAMID

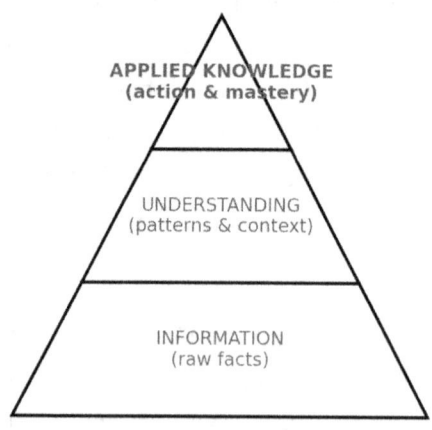

Reflection Questions:
1. Where are you stuck right now—information, understanding, or applied knowledge?
2. What one piece of knowledge, if applied, would change everything for you?

CORNERSTONE TRUTHS

1. Knowledge is the map that directs belief into mastery.
2. Ignorance is expensive, knowledge saves time, energy, and money.
3. The fastest way to grow is to model those who already excel.

REFLECTION QUESTIONS

1. Where is ignorance currently costing you?
2. What knowledge, if mastered, would multiply your results?
3. Who could you model to shorten your learning curve?

"When you grow in knowledge, you shrink the gap between where you are and where you could be."

CHAPTER THREE

CONSISTENCY: THE POWER OF DAILY ACTIONS

"We are what we repeatedly do. Excellence, then, is not an act, but a habit."

— ARISTOTLE

CONSISTENCY VS. INTENSITY

EVERYONE LOVES INTENSITY AND OFTEN OVERLOOKS consistency. Intensity is the wind through your hair – if you have any, unlike me – driving a sports car with the top down and the radio blaring your favorite music. Consistency is driving at the speed limit, wearing a seat belt, and keeping the radio low enough to have a normal conversation.

In a marriage, intensity could be the sex at night, and consistency could be having coffee with your soulmate early in the morning, before the kids wake up, being grateful for each other, and discussing the day's events. Intensity is making a phenomenal catch in the end zone to win a football game, while consistency is showing up for practice every day, catching hundreds of balls a day.

I get it. I love intensity. I also love the friends that often come with it; surprise, motivation, and emotion. It's one of life's great treasures. It's what creates many life-long memories. It's what makes movies worth watching and books worth reading.

But as much as I love intensity, you can't build a foundation on it. You can't build anything long-term on it, because no matter what it is, whatever it is that's intense, if you do it consistently intensely, it will lose its identity and become... consistency.

Intensity can only work as a cameo in a movie, not the star. Intensity creates spikes, but consistency creates identity.

Consistency is the invisible superpower that turns belief and knowledge into results. It's not what you do once that changes your life, it's what you do repeatedly. A single workout doesn't make you fit. A single act of kindness doesn't transform a relationship. A single sale doesn't build a business. But repeated daily actions, compounded over time, move mountains. Belief is the ignition key, knowledge is the map, but consistency is the fuel. Without it, the engine sputters and stalls. With it, the journey continues, sometimes slowly, sometimes painfully, but always forward.

THE PROOF OF CONSISTENCY

Geologists talk about terrain that was pretty much solid rock millions of years ago. Over millions of years, through continuous erosion aided by uplift, sediment, and gravity, everything changed. Not through intensity, but through consistency, the river kept moving – day after day, year after year – wearing the rock down inch by inch. The Colorado River did over time what no single force could accomplish in one intense moment.

What once seemed impossible slowly became inevitable. The rock yielded. Today, the world stands in awe of the natural wonder known as the Grand Canyon.

Farmers also understand and utilize the power of consistency. They don't plant seeds one day and expect a harvest the next. They tend daily, water regularly, and protect patiently. They don't do this because they love to, though many do; they do it for the harvest. To them, the harvest is their reward of consistent cultivation.

What you need to understand is that in the course of our lives, our harvests depend on the same principle – our rewards are the results and byproducts of our consistency.

Why consistency? Because greatness is never built in one moment, it is stacked brick by brick. Every great achievement is the result of thousands of consistent actions.

This is no secret, so why don't more people practice being consistent? Because it's not sexy. It's not thrilling. It doesn't take your breath away. It's not intense. It's not new. People crave novelty. People would spend more time searching for a shortcut than it would take to complete the task.

Our culture in America is hooked on instant gratification. We don't just want, we *NEED* our fast food, lightning-fast internet, streaming apps, and drop shipping. We have been ingrained with a need for immediate gratification. Why leave the house when you can buy something online? Why go out to eat when you can pay for Uber Eats and someone delivers the food right to your door? We love things fast and easy.

Consistency, on the other hand, demands discipline, a word that too many people don't like. Most people abandon their ideas even before they manifest them when they realize it's going to take discipline and consistency to get it going.

That's why they're not champions. That's right, I said it. They won't be remembered. They won't ever know what it's like to build a business that sustains entire families. They'll never have a hand in the Christmas presents under other people's trees. They're so scared of consistent discipline that they quit before they start.

Others start but lack the patience to see things through. Consider the bamboo plant. For years after planting, nothing seems to happen. You water it, nurture it, and see no growth above ground. Then suddenly, in a matter of weeks, it shoots up to 80 feet. The growth was invisible until it became undeniable. Consistency works the same way, results often lag behind actions, but when they arrive, they arrive explosively. The thing is this, while there was no growth on the outside, the plant was growing on the inside, getting a good hold of earth and rock so that when it stood tall it would remain standing.

Kobe Bryant embodied consistency. He was infamous for arriving at the gym hours before practice, working through lonely, repetitive drills. His consistency wasn't glamorous; it was sweaty, exhausting, and monotonous. But with every repetition, a neural pathway formed, and by game time, his mastery looked effortless. Behind every highlight reel moment were thousands of unseen hours of consistent practice.

When Kobe played in the Olympics in 2008, his teammates went out the night before and stayed out late. They arrived at the hotel as Kobe was leaving.

"Where are you going?" One of them asked.

"I'm gonna work out," Kobe said, as if it should have been a given. "What about y'all?" He asked.

"We need to get some sleep." One of them answered.

"Ya, that'll make us better." He chastised condescendingly.

Two days later, everyone on the team was getting up early with Kobe to work out. The late-night shenanigans stopped, and consistent discipline took over. Almost every player on that team attributes that one moment to one of the main reasons why they – dubbed The Redeem Team – won the gold.

Michael Jordan's teammates would find him drenched in sweat before practice began. His consistency built his legend as much as his talent did.

Tom Brady didn't dominate the NFL because he was the fastest, strongest, or most naturally gifted quarterback. He dominated because of consistency. His training, diet, sleep, and preparation routines became legendary. While others celebrated in the off-season, Brady was in the film room, in the gym, and on the practice field. His TB12 method wasn't a gimmick; it was a system of repeatable habits that allowed him to play at an elite level well into his forties. Champions aren't made in the spotlight; they're forged in consistency when no one is watching. Brady's legacy proves that greatness is never about one big game; it's about thousands of small, disciplined choices stacked together over time.

LeBron James invests millions of dollars annually in his body through training, diet, and recovery. His longevity is not luck; it is consistency embodied. Love him or hate him, his presence in the NBA is undeniable, largely due to his consistency.

Usain Bolt once said, "I trained four years to run nine seconds, and people give up after two months because they don't see results." This truth captures the power of consistency, the unseen years that create moments of brilliance.

Jeff Bezos built Amazon on the power of consistent focus. Day after day, the company prioritized customer experience, logistics, and scalability. While competitors pursued quick wins, Amazon built systems of consistency. That relentless execution transformed a garage startup into a global empire.

Starbucks didn't become iconic because of extraordinary coffee alone—it became iconic because of consistent customer experience. No matter where you go in the world, you know what you'll get. Consistency breeds trust, and trust builds legacy.

Warren Buffett reads for hours daily, compounding knowledge consistently. His fortune grew not through single strokes of genius, but through disciplined, repetitive choices that compounded over decades.

J.K. Rowling wrote Harry Potter not in one rush of genius but in consistent sessions at cafes. Her pen moved daily, often through rejection and hardship.

Thomas Edison tested thousands of filaments before creating the light bulb. Consistency turned repeated failure into eventual success.

Pablo Picasso produced more than 50,000 works of art. Not every piece was a masterpiece, but his consistency created genius.

Stephen King writes every day, even on holidays. His consistency opened the floodgates for creativity. Inspiration visits those who show up daily.

Nelson Mandela, in prison for 27 years, never abandoned consistency. He exercised daily, studied daily, and reflected daily. When freedom came, his consistent character gave him credibility to unify a nation.

Gandhi practiced daily rituals of prayer and fasting. His consistent alignment of word and deed made him unshakable.

HOW TO BUILD CONSISTENCY

In NLP, consistency is how you reprogram your subconscious. Every repeated action tells your brain, 'This is who I am.' Miss too many repetitions, and your identity weakens. Keep repeating, and your identity strengthens.

Anchoring helps cement consistency. Attach new habits to existing ones, drink water after brushing your teeth, and read after your morning coffee. Reframing helps too, see consistency not as an obligation, but as empowerment. "I get to grow stronger today," instead of "I have to work out."

What if you treated consistency as sacred? Imagine committing to 30 minutes of learning daily. In one year, that's 182 hours, nearly a full semester. What if you saved a small amount every day? Over decades, wealth would accumulate effortlessly. What if you expressed one word of gratitude daily? In time, your relationships would transform completely.

What if you became the person known for always showing up? Imagine how your reputation would grow. People don't trust sporadic brilliance—they trust reliability.

What if you practiced one consistent action in each of the seven life areas: health, wealth, relationships, vocation, spirituality, social impact, and mindset? Over time, you would not only succeed but also achieve balance and fulfillment.

I was thirteen the first time my mom took me to the gym. I fell in love instantly. The weights, the grind, the sweat — it clicked. Strength didn't come as a gift. It came through consistency. Show up, lift, rest, repeat. That rhythm became my foundation.

By high school, that consistency had carried me onto the football field. For me, football was also love at first sight. Where else can you hit someone as hard as you can, and they thank you for it? Coaches praised me for being an animal on the field, but what they were really praising was my consistency. Every squat, every sprint, every late-night lift stacked up and showed on game day.

At the same time, my dad's work ethic was pounding into me from another direction. While friends partied, I worked. While others slept in, I trained. I made myself a promise: nobody would ever outwork me. Not in the gym. Not on the job. Not anywhere.

I had dreams of playing professional football. Colleges noticed. Offers came in. But the risk was real, if I got hurt, my family had no safety net. Besides, there was no way we could cover the tuition. That reality forced me to make a choice I would prefer not to have made. Instead of chasing the dream, I stepped into my trade. It wasn't glamorous; there were no Friday Night Lights, there were no intense speeches, headbutts with teammates while we worked ourselves into a frenzy, no roar of the crowd... but it was consistent. I woke up every day early, with my father's voice ringing in my ears, "It's time to catch the bad guys!" And I worked, and I learned, and I perfected, and I surpassed expectations, and I set new ones, and I surpassed those. Brick by brick, I built.

There were plenty of moments along the way when I thought about giving up. Long days, missed opportunities, the grind with no immediate payoff. But I knew what consistency had already taught me: if you keep putting one foot in front of the other, eventually you get somewhere no one else does.

When I started karate in my thirties, I brought the same approach with me. I wasn't the biggest. I wasn't the tallest. I certainly wasn't the most limber – hell, I couldn't even touch my toes without bending my knees! But I knew I could be the most consistent. That's what carried me through eight-hour black belt tests designed to break you physically and mentally. When exhaustion screamed at me to stop, consistency whispered: *Just one more step. Just one more punch. Just one more round.*

Today I'm a second-degree black belt. Not because of talent. Not because of shortcuts. But because consistency has always been my superpower. I've lived my entire life by this truth: while others quit, I keep going. And that has made all the difference between me getting up every day and just working, or me working on this book to offer you guidance and support.

"Consistency beats talent, size, and circumstance. It's the superpower anyone can choose."

Picture yourself one year from now. You've stuck with one small habit daily writing 500 words, meditating 10 minutes, or making one call. Day by day it felt ordinary, but by year's end, you've written a book, transformed your mind, or grown your business.

Picture yourself five years from now. You chose one consistent habit in health, one in wealth, one in relationships, and one in spirit. Every day you showed up. Five years later, you're fit, financially secure, deeply connected, and spiritually grounded.

THE CONSISTENCY STAIRCASE

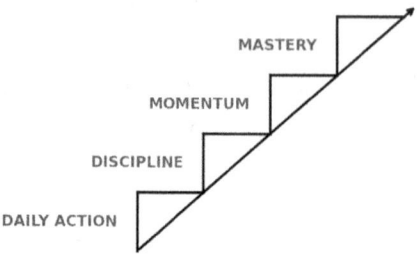

Reflection Questions:
1. What's one step you've been avoiding?
2. What small action, done daily, would move you toward mastery?

CORNERSTONE TRUTHS

1. Consistency is the bridge between belief and results.
2. Small daily actions, compounded over time, create transformation.
3. Habits are highways in the brain—consistency builds them.

REFLECTION QUESTIONS

1. Where have you quit too early in the past?
2. What one habit, if practiced daily, would transform your life?
3. How can you anchor this habit to something you already do?

Consistency is the compound interest of success — small deposits daily, exponential results over time.

CHAPTER FOUR

RESULTS: THE PROOF
OF PERSISTENCE

"You can't argue with results. They tell the story of what was truly done."

— ANONYMOUS

THE PROOF IS IN THE PUDDING

RESULTS ARE THE SCOREBOARD OF LIFE. THEY ARE THE tangible proof of your belief, knowledge, and consistency. You can have the strongest belief, the deepest knowledge, and the most disciplined consistency, but at some point, the question becomes: What did all of that produce?

Results are the fruit of the seeds you've sown, the harvest after months of labor, the numbers on the scoreboard after the game. They don't lie, they don't flatter, they don't care about excuses, and they don't care about your feelings.

A farmer can tell himself all season long that he worked hard, but when harvest comes, the fields reveal the truth. Either there is grain, or there is not. Results remove illusion. Results chop down lies at the knees. Results mirror back action, reaction, and non-action. They cut through stories and opinions and reveal the facts of what was truly done. In other words, results are irrefutable truths.

Why? Because they provide feedback. They show you whether your current strategy is working or failing. Results are reality's way of answering unanswered questions. Without results, you drift into fantasy, believing effort alone is enough. Of course, effort matters, but only results show whether the effort was applied effectively.

Too many people confuse movement for progress. They confuse being busy with being effective. I have told my sales team over and over again that the character Pig Pen, in the Charlie Brown cartoons, always seemed busy. When many characters were in one shot, Charlie, Linus, Lucy, Snoopy, and the others had to stand a short distance from Pig Pen because of the flurry of activity surrounding him. BUT HE NEVER DID ANYTHING!

Two people can make the same number of calls, can get to the job site at the same time, can go to the gym the same amount of time – but always get different results.

One sales call will make 100 calls to try to make a sale, while another will make 100 calls to meet a quota. One person can get to the job site prepared and right to work, while another can have issues with a wife or girl-friend and spend 4 hours on the phone. One goes to the gym pumped up, ready to work, while the other can go socialize and talk to girls. Either way, the results will show who created movement and who created progress.

Why not results? Because when pursued in isolation, they can mislead. Results without context can cause pride or despair. One success can make you complacent; one failure can make you quit. Results matter, but they must be framed as feedback, not final judgment.

Results are like a mirror. They reflect back what you put in. Sometimes the reflection is flattering; other times it is sobering. But the mirror is neutral; it doesn't distort. If you want a different reflection, you don't smash the mirror; you change what stands before it.

For business owners, the mirror is the results. For employees, the mirror can be their annual review. When people get good or great reviews, they leave the office smiling, shaking hands, and thanking their supervisor or boss for the kind words. They love what they "saw" and get back to work, hoping to see more of the same the following year. Then there are those who get a bad review and, instead of understanding why they're being criticized, their weakness tries to protect them and they feel attacked.

Emotion gets stirred up, and sometimes angry words are said. "So, that's it?" You're firing me? I've been here for ten years. Ten years! And now you're firing me?" They'll scream.

The supervisor would put his hands out, "Hey, hey, take it easy. I didn't say anything about firing you. I'm just telling you what you need to do to produce better results."

But the worker leaves and tells whoever will listen that the supervisor hates him, is jealous of him, or a bunch of other reasons he feels he isn't being given a fair shot. "I don't know why, but he hates me!"

Results are the scoreboard in sports. A player can say he feels like he's winning, but the scoreboard settles the matter. The beauty of results is their objectivity. They give clarity where emotion gives confusion.

Take Michael Phelps, the most decorated Olympian in history. His belief in himself and his knowledge of swimming technique were essential, but the results, 23 gold medals cemented his legacy. Results were the public proof of years of private persistence.

Consider Tom Brady. Drafted as the 199th pick, his belief was unshakable, his consistency legendary. But it was results, seven Super Bowl rings, that silenced critics and carved his place as the greatest quarterback of all time.

In business, results determine survival. *If you're a business owner, you might want to read the previous sentence again.* Steve Jobs was fired from Apple despite his vision, knowledge, and belief because, at the time, the company's results faltered. When he returned years later, his persistence produced results: the iPod, iPhone, and iPad, which revived Apple and transformed culture itself.

Elon Musk is often criticized for his eccentricity, but the results make his voice undeniable. Electric cars on highways, reusable rockets in the sky, these results drown out the noise of doubt. Love him or hate him, the scoreboard is visible to all.

J.K. Rowling faced dozens of rejections before a publisher finally accepted Harry Potter. Her persistence mattered, but what changed her life were the results— books sold, children reading, a cultural phenomenon born. The results gave her story weight beyond belief and persistence alone.

Martin Luther King Jr. delivered countless speeches, led marches, and endured opposition. But the Civil Rights Act of 1964 was the result that cemented his legacy. It wasn't just words; it was change codified into law. The results are evidence of leadership fulfilled.

In NLP, results are treated as feedback. Failure is not a dead end; it is information. If your current approach is not producing results, the solution is not to quit but to change your strategy. Results reveal the adjustments needed for progress.

This reframing transforms failure into fuel. Instead of asking, 'Why didn't it work?' you ask, 'What can I learn from this?' Results become teachers rather than verdicts.

What if you stopped ignoring results? How much money would you save if you faced financial truth rather than hiding behind stories? What if you measured the health results of your habits honestly? How different would your body feel a year from now? What if you tracked the emotional climate of your family, measuring whether your actions brought connection or distance? Facing results directly is uncomfortable, but it is liberating.

What if you measured results across all seven areas of life? What if every quarter you asked: Am I healthier, wealthier, wiser, more connected, more purposeful, more spiritual, more impactful? Such clarity would cut through confusion and provide a compass for growth.

Thomas Edison failed thousands of times before creating a working light bulb. He reframed those results: 'I have not failed. I've just found 10,000 ways that won't work.' His genius was not just invention; it was persistence plus reframing results as progress.

The Wright brothers faced ridicule, crashes, and public doubt. But the moment their plane lifted off, results changed everything. From doubted dreamers to aviation pioneers—the scoreboard was undeniable.

When I first started my business, there were months where it felt like I was pouring everything in and getting scraps out. Long days in the field, late nights on the books, and what seemed like endless problems. Some weeks, I questioned whether it was worth it. My mind kept offering me ways out – I'm young – I need more experience – maybe I should work for someone else for five years and try again – a salary sure would reduce my anxiety level about money.

But I refused to quit. I just kept stacking one day on top of the next. I kept knocking on doors, taking calls, fixing problems, and building a reputation one job at a time.

Then, one afternoon, I sat across from my accountant, and he looked up at me with a grin. "You know you just crossed a million in revenue, right?"

It hit me like a Hulk Clap. A million dollars! Me? After I told him not to joke around and he assured me he wasn't joking, I sat back, and an overwhelming feeling of accomplishment washed over me. It wasn't a dream. It wasn't a one-of-these-days. It wasn't an idea. There were 7 digits on the bank sheet, separated by two commas.

That was the moment I understood the power of results. The grind, the persistence, the daily unseen work, all of it had crystallized into something undeniable. Goals written down were just writing, what some might've thought was wishful thinking, but the results made it real.

"Persistence is invisible until results make it visible."

But not every result feels good. Some of them sting.

I remember the year I ignored my financial discipline and overextended the business. I thought hustle alone would outrun mistakes. Instead, the numbers hit me like a hammer. Cash flow was tight. Debt piled up. I had to face a result I couldn't spin; the business was bleeding because of my decisions.

For a while, shame weighed heavily on me. I could have called it failure. But results don't lie, they teach. That hard season forced me to confront what I didn't want to face: hustle without structure is a time bomb. It forced me to get serious about financial controls, pricing models, and decision-making discipline.

What felt like a disaster became a turning point. The result wasn't failure, it was feedback. And that feedback changed the trajectory of my business forever.

"Hard results are not punishment. They are feedback."

Results are like fruit. You can water a tree, fertilize it, and believe it will grow. But eventually, it must bear fruit. A barren tree tells the truth. In life, results are the fruit of your actions. The harvest cannot be faked. If you want sweeter fruit, you must change the soil, the seeds, or the sun exposure—not complain about the harvest.

Imagine yourself one year from now, having measured results every month. You know exactly where you stand in your finances, health, relationships, and spirit. Instead of living in vague hope, you live with clarity. You know what to change and what to reinforce. That clarity is power.

Now picture five years from now. Each year you tracked and adjusted based on results. You didn't ignore data—you embraced it. The compounding effect of truth-telling turned small adjustments into massive outcomes. Results became your ally, not your enemy.

NLP teaches the value of SMART outcomes, Specific, Measurable, Achievable, Relevant, and Time-bound. By framing goals this way, you invite measurable results. For example: 'I will increase my income by 20% in 12 months by closing 5 new clients per month.' Such clarity transforms vague desires into measurable progress.

You can't reverse-engineer a vague goal. Only when you set the target can you consciously and intelligently plan on how to get there. If a billionaire says he wants to do go mars, once his mind is made up, he thinks about the information he needs, the people he needs, the location, etc. he shares the belief to others who buy in, invests in the knowledge, get it going – it fails, but some parts worked, so they keep that intact and rework the reasons why it failed, each time getting closer to space.

When results are specific and tracked, your subconscious works like a heat-seeking missile, adjusting behavior until the target is hit. This alignment between vision and measurable action accelerates achievement.

Consider Miyamoto Musashi. His belief and training were relentless, but it was results, more than sixty duels fought and never lost, that defined his greatness. The world doesn't remember how many hours he practiced alone in the mountains or how many forms he repeated with his wooden sword. They remember the victories, the battles where his skill and discipline were tested under pressure and proved undeniable. Results became the public face of his private persistence. His legacy isn't built on the theory of mastery; it's built on the undeniable evidence of outcomes.

THE RESULTS BULLSEYE

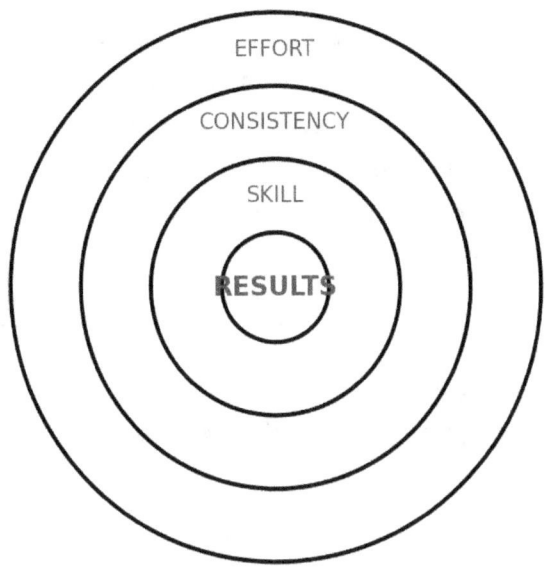

EFFORT

CONSISTENCY

SKILL

RESULTS

Reflection Questions:
1. What's the "bullseye result" you're aiming for right now?
2. What layers of effort must you stack to reach it?

CORNERSTONE TRUTHS

1. Results are the scoreboard of persistence—they reveal the truth without bias.
2. Results should be treated as feedback, not final judgment.
3. Results, tracked across life's seven areas, provide clarity and compass.

REFLECTION QUESTIONS

1. Where in your life are you ignoring results because they make you uncomfortable?
2. What small adjustment could you make right now based on results you're seeing?
3. How could you begin measuring results in all seven areas of life?

"Results don't lie—they reflect. They tell you not who you are forever, but who you've been consistently."

PART TWO
THE SEVEN PILLARS
OF LIFE MASTERY

"Balance is not something you find, it's something you create."

— TIM GROVER

With the Cornerstones secure, we can now build upward into the seven great pillars of human experience: Physical, Mental, Spiritual, Familial, Social, Vocational, and Financial. Each is a vital arena, and together they form a complete life. In this part, you'll see how the Four Cornerstones express themselves differently in each area. You'll also discover that when one area weakens, the others feel the strain, but when one is strengthened, the others are lifted. This is where your blueprint begins to take shape in every dimension of life.

CHAPTER FIVE

PHYSICAL: FOUNDATION OF ENERGY AND VITALITY

"Take care of your body. It's the only place you have to live."

— JIM ROHN

THE SCIENCE BEHIND PHYSICAL HEALTH

YOUR PHYSICAL BODY IS THE FOUNDATION FOR EVERYTHING you will ever do in this life. It is the vehicle that carries you through every challenge, every victory, every relationship, and every opportunity. You can have the sharpest mind, the deepest belief, and the greatest ambitions, but without a healthy body to sustain them, your dreams will remain limited by fatigue, illness, or lack of vitality.

Think of your body as the engine of a high-performance car. Belief is the driver, knowledge is the map, consistency is the maintenance routine, but without fuel and a finely tuned engine, the car goes nowhere. The body either empowers or restricts every other life pursuit.

I can tell you how this happens, but I've learned that when someone is being told something, it doesn't last nearly as long as when someone is explaining something, because the person, even if it's for a short time, understands it. From there, the belief slips into the subconscious, so even though someone can't articulate why he feels a certain way, he just knows that he does. So with that in mind, let's step into the Mind Lab for a brief moment.

Biologically speaking, taking care of your body through exercise does three things, and those three things do many other things.

1. It releases Dopamine, which is a crucial neurotransmitter in the brain. It regulates motivation, reward, movement, learning, and attention. It drives goal-directed behaviors by making pleasurable activities feel good and motivating us to repeat them!
2. It releases Serotonin, another transmitter in the brain. This one regulates mood, happiness, and emotional stability. It also influences sleep, appetite, digestion, memory, and social behavior with balanced levels promoting focus and

calmness. When the serotonin is unbalanced, it links to depression and anxiety.

3. It releases Brain-Derived Neurotrophic Factor (BDFN). This is a protein that acts like fertilizer for the brain, promoting neuron growth (which makes you capable of learning more), survival, and connections with others. It also deeply impacts overall body chemistry.

ENERGY

Why take care of the body? Because energy is life. A strong, healthy body multiplies everything else you do. When your body is aligned, your mind is sharper, your emotions steadier, and your spirit freer. Why not? Because neglect feels easier in the moment. Skipping exercise, indulging in junk food, or sacrificing sleep for productivity feels convenient now, but each act of neglect withdraws from your future capacity. Eventually, the debt comes due.

There's good energy and bad energy, and regardless of who you are, you are going to give and get both of them. The empowering thing is, you get to choose. Don't you hate being around the type of people who can have a great day, but one little thing ruins the rest of their day? They bring their negativity around you, and you hate being there – you think 'OMG, is this what the entire day is going to be like with this guy?' Then you get home and don't know why, but you start complaining about things around the house.

I just want to say something to my work-complainers reading this book – it never makes the work go any faster! In fact, it does the opposite. People with good energy make work feel effortless. People that bitch and moan work slowly and poorly.

Good energy people find solutions to unexpected problems, not another reason to gripe. Have you ever been with someone who laughs off everything and stays in a good mood, and after a day with him, you go home, and you're a little more playful? The reason is that energy transmits. If you don't guard your good energy, it could be affected by someone with bad energy.

Your body is your temple. Neglect it, and the structure weakens. Honor it, and it becomes a sanctuary. Your body is also your vehicle. Fail to maintain it, and it breaks down prematurely. Care for it, and it carries you further than you imagined.

Like a bank account, you make deposits and withdrawals. Healthy choices deposit energy; poor choices withdraw it. Ignore the balance for too long, and you risk bankruptcy, disease, exhaustion, or a crisis that could have been avoided. Invest daily, and the account compounds into longevity and vitality.

VITALITY

An online dictionary defines the word as – *the state of being strong and active – the power giving continuance of life, present in all living things.* My personal definition is an awakening sense of feeling fully alive. Like when you jump into cold water, the rush of speeding on a motorcycle down a winding mountain, winning a foot race, feeling you can climb any mountain, cross any water, and even fly if you absolutely had to. Vitality is energy at its best. It bleeds into success, likeability, engagement, and longevity.

Consider LeBron James, who invests millions annually in his body through training, nutrition, and recovery. His career longevity is not luck; it is the compounding of daily investments in his physical foundation.

Tom Brady played in the NFL well into his 40s, not because of raw talent alone, but because of relentless focus on diet, flexibility, and recovery. He proved that mastery of the physical body extends performance far beyond what most believe possible.

But it's not just elite athletes. Think of someone who decided to walk 30 minutes every day. Within a year, they lost weight, gained confidence, and extended their life expectancy. The transformation wasn't built on dramatic bursts, but on consistent physical care.

A mother of three once committed to drinking more water and walking daily for just 20 minutes. Two years later, she was 60 pounds lighter, off medications, and had the energy to play with her kids. Her story shows that consistency in small habits compounds into extraordinary results.

In NLP, changing how we relate to health behaviors can transform outcomes. Reframing exercise from 'punishment for eating' to 'celebration of movement' shifts emotion from dread to joy. Anchoring can lock in habits; listening to a specific empowering playlist every time you work out associates the music with vitality.

Submodalities refer to the specific qualities or fine distinctions within our primary senses, such as sound, sight, and touch; like brightness, size, or volume, which code our experiences and memories in NLP and psychology. If someone were to use their submodalities to shrink the image of a bad memory, it could alter its emotional impact. It can also shift cravings. Imagine seeing unhealthy food in dull, gray images while amplifying the colors and sounds of vibrant, healthy meals. Your brain begins to code preferences differently, making healthier choices more appealing at the subconscious level.

Anchoring and stacking habits work especially well for physical mastery. For example, anchoring stretching to brushing your teeth ensures flexibility becomes automatic. Stacking water intake with every meal builds hydration into daily life without effort. NLP reframing of internal dialogue, changing 'I'm too tired to work out' into 'Movement will energize me', reshapes resistance into motivation.

What if you treated your body as your greatest asset? What if every day you nourished it, trained it, and rested it as though your future depended on it? Because it does. How would your energy change if you slept eight quality hours each night? How would your confidence shift if you were proud of how your body felt and looked? How much more influence could you command if you radiated vitality when you walked into a room?

What if you ignored your body for another decade? What would the cost be? More doctor's visits, medications, and restrictions? How would neglecting your body affect your children, your spouse, your mission? The what-if cuts both ways, vitality or decline, by daily choice.

Steve Jobs once said, 'Your time is limited, so don't waste it living someone else's life.' His battle with illness reminds us that health is the ultimate wealth. All the vision in the world cannot overcome a failing body. His story is a sobering reminder that vitality cannot be purchased at the last moment, it must be invested in daily.

Mahatma Gandhi demonstrated that mastery of the body could serve a higher mission. Through fasting and discipline, he turned his physical choices into a source of moral power. His body became a vessel for influence far beyond himself.

Tony Robbins, known for his immense energy on stage, maintains that energy through strict routines of diet, supplementation, and exercise. His global influence is fueled by physical vitality he deliberately protects.

I still remember the first time I took my training seriously again as an adult. I'd always loved the gym since I was a teenager, but there came a point in my thirties when I realized the weight room wasn't just about muscles, it was about energy.

When I committed to a new routine, lifting consistently, dialing in my diet, and making recovery as important as work, I noticed something wild. It wasn't just my body that changed. My energy at work skyrocketed. I walked into meetings sharper. I could grind through long days without crashing. My leadership felt more present, because I wasn't dragging my body like a weight behind me.

At home, it was even bigger. My kids didn't just see a dad, they saw an example. I could chase them, wrestle with them, play with them, and still have fuel in the tank. That was what we could all see on the outside, but, like most things at home, whether good or bad, there are ripple effects. The added fun times with them also helped them open up to me more. They were more present in conversations when I was giving 'Dad' advice; their presence led to more questions, which made it easier for me to be more patient with them and to explain my views until they understood them.

My wife could feel the difference, too. I was better rested, less snappy, more empathetic, less of a shoulder-shrugger, I laughed louder, and was more carefree rather than introspective and in my head. Confidence in your body shows up in the way you carry yourself in every relationship.

That season taught me this: caring for your body is never selfish. It's a gift to everyone who depends on you.

"When your body thrives, every area of life rises with it."

But I've also learned the hard way what happens when you neglect your body.

There was a stretch in my late twenties where I was so focused on building the business that I told myself I didn't have time to train. I skipped workouts, ate like garbage, and took no responsibility for it because I was 'always on the run,' and burned the candle at both ends. At first, I thought I was buying time. In reality, I was draining it.

The truth showed up quickly. I was exhausted by noon. My patience with my team and my family wore thin. Stress piled up faster because I didn't have an outlet. And the mirror wasn't lying either, the confidence I once carried in my body slipped away.

The wake-up call came when even simple things felt hard. Walking into a 14-hour workday without energy isn't a strength. It's a slow bleed. I realized that my body was the engine of everything I wanted to build, and I was neglecting the very machine that carried me.

That season burned this lesson into me: you don't get to ignore your body and escape the consequences. Eventually, the bill comes due.

We are all given the opportunity to neglect our bodies; everything from time constraints, physical injuries, chronic conditions, family responsibilities, looming deadlines, travel or commute – the list goes on and on. But remember, the mirror doesn't care about your reasons; it'll just show you the data.

"Neglect your body, and it will neglect you back."

Your body is the foundation of a house. You can decorate the rooms with success, fill them with relationships, and build upper levels of purpose. But if the foundation cracks, everything else is at risk. Build the body strong, and the house stands firm through storms.

What if you aligned physical mastery with all seven areas of life?

- In health: daily exercise builds vitality.
- In wealth: health prevents costly medical crises.
- In relationships: energy lets you show up fully.
- In vocation: strength sustains long work and focus.

- In spirit: clarity grows when the body is balanced.
- In social impact: vitality inspires others.
- In mindset: discipline in body sharpens discipline in thought.

Picture yourself at 80, vibrant, mobile, and mentally sharp. Imagine looking back, knowing it wasn't luck but consistency that built this vitality. Picture yourself running with your grandchildren, traveling, and pursuing passions. That future is not built at 80, it is built daily in your 30s, 40s, and 50s.

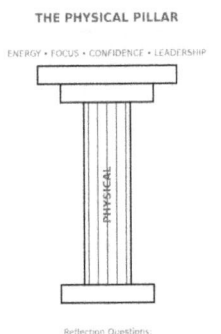

THE PHYSICAL PILLAR

ENERGY • FOCUS • CONFIDENCE • LEADERSHIP

PHYSICAL

Reflection Questions:
1. How does your current physical state support—or limit—your life?
2. What one daily practice would strengthen your "pillar"?

Picture an alternate future: struggling with preventable disease, regretting choices, wishing for time back. Both futures are possible, your daily decisions choose the path.

CORNERSTONE TRUTHS

1. The body is the foundation of energy and vitality.
2. Every other pursuit is limited or empowered by physical health.
3. Daily deposits in health compound into longevity and influence.

REFLECTION QUESTIONS

1. Where are you neglecting your body today, and what is it costing you?
2. What one daily habit could you start now to increase vitality?
3. How would mastering your body ripple into your family, business, and mission?

"Your body is the foundation of your legacy—build it strong, and it will carry you far."

CHAPTER SIX

MENTAL: THE ARCHITECT OF REALITY

"The mind is everything. What you think you become."

— BUDDHA

YOUR MIND IS THE ARCHITECT OF YOUR REALITY. BEFORE any result shows up in your life, it first exists as a thought, an image, or a belief within the mind. The body is the foundation, but the mind is the blueprint that guides what gets built upon it. Every invention, every achievement, every movement in history began as an idea, shaped and directed by the human mind.

The mind is both a lens and a filter. It does not simply record reality; it interprets it, assigns meaning to it, and then directs behavior in response. Your world is not shaped by what happens to you but by how your mind chooses to perceive it. Two people can face the same circumstance; one sees opportunity, the other sees defeat. The difference lies not in the circumstance but in the architecture of the mind.

Why master the mind? Because thoughts precede actions, and actions precede destiny. The quality of your thinking determines the quality of your life. Your brain physically rewires itself based on your thought patterns through a process called neuroplasticity.

I want you to know this very important truth: it will give you all the reason in the world to control your thoughts. Thoughts come unbidden into our brains, as do fear, worry, anxiety, etc. We can't help that. But every thought that you entertain repeatedly carves neural pathways – like water cutting grooves into stone, the way the Colorado River caused the Grand Canyon. If you entertain a limiting thought 10,000 times, you will build a superhighway to that conclusion. Your brain will accept it as fact and will build up military-style defenses to protect those thoughts.

This is how two entrepreneurs can attend the same two-day conference – one leaves energized with three business ideas and four new connections, while the other leaves with nothing. Same conference. Same industry. Same-sized companies. But the difference is the mental filters; it's how their minds have been trained to perceive their limits.

Your thoughts trigger neurochemical responses. I mentioned in the previous chapter the benefits of releasing dopamine and serotonin, but not all chemicals are good. Thoughts of fear, anxiety, and self-doubt flood your system with cortisol. If you didn't know, cortisol is the primary stress hormone, and its presence throughout your system can have a wide range of immediate and long-term effects.

A well-trained mind generates clarity, creativity, and resilience. However, left unchecked, the mind can be a tyrant. It will invent fears, magnify doubts, and trap you in cycles of limitation. It's neglected, unmastered, and undisciplined. It builds personal prisons instead of palaces.

Let me be specific about what a neglected or unmastered mind costs you:

1. Decision-making: an unmastered mind overreacts to the latest crisis. The chance that something can go wrong prevents you from taking risks that are necessary for growth. You make quick, rash, impulsive decisions based on emotions disguised as logic and experience.

2. Relationships: Your mind invents meanings and narratives about what others have meant and how they think of you. You react to stories made up in your head, not to reality. You see what you want to see, not what's in front of you. Instead of asking for clarity, you punch, thinking you're punching back, when no one has swung at you. You let go of good relationships (partners,

employees, consultants) easily, but fight to keep bad ones.

3. Health: Chronic stress from unmanaged, debilitating, limited thoughts literally accelerates aging by shortening your telomeres (the protective caps on your DNA)

4. Wealth: Unchecked, limited thinking keeps you playing small. You see coaching as an expense, not an asset. You see conferences as a waste of time when you could be working. As a result, your income rarely exceeds the self-concept you allow to live in your mind.

Think of the mind as an operating system. If it is corrupted with viruses, fear, doubt, or limiting beliefs, everything built upon it malfunctions. But when upgraded with empowering beliefs, clarity of vision, and intentional focus, the entire system runs with precision and power.

Or consider the mind as an architect's blueprint. Without a clear plan, construction falters. A strong foundation may exist, but without a mental design, the building becomes chaotic. Blueprints shape reality. Your mental images, what you picture consistently, become the structures of your life.

Albert Einstein once said, 'Imagination is more important than knowledge.' His breakthroughs were born not from mechanical repetition but from creative leaps of mind. He visualized riding on beams of light before he proved relativity mathematically. The blueprint of his mind shaped modern physics.

Consider Bruce Lee. He was more than a martial artist, he was a philosopher of the mind. Lee believed the greatest fight was not in the ring but in the mind. Long before Hollywood accepted him, he saw himself as a global icon, bridging East and West. His mental pillar was unshakable: visualization, affirmations, and a relentless focus on self-mastery. He trained his thoughts as rigorously as his body, refusing to be trapped by limiting beliefs. His famous words still echo: *"As you think, so shall you become."* His mind built the stage of his life long before the world caught up.

Viktor Frankl, imprisoned in Nazi concentration camps, discovered that the last of human freedoms was the ability to choose one's attitude. Even amidst horror, his mind created meaning, and that meaning gave him the strength to survive and later to inspire millions.

Every great artist, from Leonardo da Vinci to Maya Angelou, lived first in the theater of their mind. The canvas, the page, the stage, all were reflections of inner vision. The mind conceives, then the hands create.

In NLP, the mind is seen as a map of perception rather than a mirror of reality. Change the map, and you change your experience. Reframing is one of the most powerful tools: by shifting the meaning you assign to an event, you transform its emotional impact. For example, rejection can be reframed as redirection, failure as feedback, obstacles as opportunities. The event doesn't change, but your experience of it does.

Submodalities take this further. Every thought and memory has qualities, color, size, brightness, sound, weight. By altering these qualities, you alter the intensity of your experience. Shrink the image of a fear, drain its color, and push it far away in your mental landscape, and suddenly the fear loses its grip. Enlarge the image of your goals, brighten them, and bring them close, and motivation surges.

Meta-programs are the unconscious filters that guide how we process the world. Some people are motivated toward pleasure, others away from pain. Some focus on the big picture, others on details. By recognizing and adjusting these programs, you can redesign how your mind navigates reality.

What if you could choose your thoughts the way you choose your clothes? What if, each morning, you selected empowering beliefs, dressed yourself in gratitude, and put on a jacket of confidence? How different would your day unfold?

What if you stopped believing every thought you had? How much suffering would dissolve if you realized that not all thoughts are truth, many are echoes of fear, conditioning, or old patterns? What if you curated your thoughts as carefully as you curate your diet?

What if you deliberately constructed mental movies of your future, seeing yourself thriving in health, wealth, love, and purpose? How much faster would you move toward those realities if your mind rehearsed success every day?

Elon Musk imagines futures before others believe they are possible. Electric cars, reusable rockets, colonizing Mars, all were mental blueprints long before they were physical realities. His willingness to think expansively, despite ridicule, demonstrates the power of mind as architect.

Consider Tom Brady. Before he ever stepped on the field, he had already played the game in his mind. Brady was known for relentless film study, but it wasn't just analysis, it was mental rehearsal. He visualized defenses, practiced throws in his imagination, and walked through victory in his head long before kickoff. His mind always stepped onto the field before his body did. That mental preparation allowed him to remain calm under pressure, adapt in real time, and deliver results when it mattered most. For Brady, mindset wasn't a side tool, it was the edge that turned a sixth-round draft pick into the greatest quarterback of all time

There was a season in business when everything felt like it was crashing down at once. Jobs were delayed, a key employee quit, and cash flow was razor thin. I remember driving to work one morning with my stomach in knots, thinking, *"Why does this always happen to me?"*

That one question kept me trapped. As long as I saw myself as the victim of circumstances, the weight felt unbearable. Then a mentor dropped a line that snapped me out of it: *"What if this isn't happening to you but for you?"*

That shift in mindset changed everything. Instead of looking at setbacks as punishments, I started to see them as training. Problems became feedback. Delays became lessons. Even the cash crunch became a chance to get lean and disciplined.

The facts hadn't changed, the jobs were still delayed, the employee was still gone, the money was still tight. But my mindset reframed the entire story. Suddenly, I was no longer buried under the challenge. I was being forged by it. That reframe gave me the strength to push forward and the creativity to find solutions I would have missed if I stayed stuck in self-pity.

"Change the story in your head, and you change the power in your hands."

A few years later, I had an experience that proved the power of visualization. It was during training for my black belt test, eight hours of nonstop physical and mental endurance. The test was brutal. You don't survive it on muscle alone. You need mindset.

In the weeks leading up to it, I rehearsed every scenario in my mind. I pictured the exhaustion. I pictured my legs shaking, my lungs burning, my body screaming to quit. And then I pictured myself pushing through anyway. I pictured myself hearing the final words: *"You passed."*

When test day came, the physical pain was real. Every muscle ached. My mind tried to convince me I couldn't keep going. But I had already been there in my head. I had already fought those battles in rehearsal. And because I had rehearsed victory, I knew exactly how to respond when the real test hit.

That day ended with a belt tied around my waist and a truth burned into me forever: your body follows where your mind has already gone.

"If you can win it in your head, you can win it in the world."

Your mind is like a lens. Clean and focused, it brings clarity. Dirty and distorted, it obscures truth. The same scenery can look beautiful or bleak depending on the lens. Mastering the mind is polishing the lens daily.

WHERE ARE YOU ON THE MENTAL MASTERY CONTINUUM?

You're not always a victim, and you're not always a master – mental mastery is a continuum – it constantly moves or evolves. Most of us move along it depending on the area of life or the level of stress.

Level 1 – Metal Victim: Life happens TO you. You're controlled by outside circumstances, other people's opinions, and your up-and-down emotions. Your self-talk is like a guard talking to an unruly prisoner. You're stuck in loops of worry, resentment, or self pity.

Level 2 – Mental Awareness: You're starting to realize that there are patterns in your thinking. Not all of the time, but sometimes you catch yourself in negative spirals, but you don't know yet how to redirect or challenge them. You know your mind needs work, but you're not at the point of spending energy on finding how to get help.

Level 3 – Mental Manager: You actively manage your thoughts most days. You've learned some tools – reframing, visualization, and affirmations – and you use them often, but not always. You feel good because you can recover from setbacks faster than before. People who have never complimented you have done so.

Level 4 – Mental Architect: You're serious now. You deliberately design your mental landscape. You pick and choose your thoughts like an art collector. You respond to life from choice, not compulsion. Challenges don't scare you; they sharpen you. Your mind is a disciplined instrument.

Level 5 – Mental Master: Your mind is so trained that empowering thoughts automatically come from your core beliefs. You're unshakeable in who you are, your core identity. External chaos and happenings can affect you, but can't reach your inner peace. You live in flow.

Your presence alone elevates others. Go-getters flock to you. Lazy people, liars, thieves, and those who would stoop low for personal gain avoid you.

Be honest. Where do you see yourself? If you're not high on the list, it's okay, give yourself some pass; we could all use a little more self-grace. The purpose of showing you the levels isn't to make you feel bad; it's to help you think about where you want to be six months from now. The truth is, most people are stuck between Level 1 and 2. With consistent practice, you can reach Level 3 within 90 days – that's where real transformation begins.

But I just don't want to tell you about this beautiful place in a land far, far away, like a fairytale. I want to show you how to get there.

Here's an NLP routine for daily mental mastery:

1. Begin the day by visualizing three key outcomes you want to achieve. Make the images big, bright, and vivid.
2. Reframe potential challenges before they arise: decide in advance what they will mean to you.
3. Anchor a resourceful state—confidence, peace, or determination—by linking it to a physical gesture (like pressing thumb and finger together).
4. Throughout the day, notice your thoughts. When a disempowering one arises, shrink it, push it away, and replace it with an empowering one.

5. End the day with gratitude, rehearsing mental images of what went well.

What if you mastered your mind across all seven life areas?

- In health: reframing pain as progress could keep you consistent.
- In wealth: visualizing abundance could drive creative strategies.
- In relationships: choosing empowering meanings could heal conflicts.
- In vocation: focus on vision could sustain persistence.
- In spirit: meditation could open deeper clarity.
- In social impact: reframing obstacles as stepping stones could amplify influence.
- In mindset itself: curating thoughts would unlock peace and power.

Picture yourself one year from now, having mastered the architecture of your mind. You wake with clarity, choose empowering meanings, and move through challenges with resilience. Imagine the compounding effect after five years—your mind so disciplined and intentional that reality bends to its vision. You become the deliberate designer of your destiny.

Now picture the opposite: a mind left unchecked. Thoughts run wild, fears dictate choices, doubts kill dreams. The blueprint of the mind builds prisons of

limitation. This too is possible
—but avoidable with mastery.

THE MENTAL PILLAR

VISION • CLARITY • FOCUS

MENTAL

Reflection Questions:
1. What mindset shift would give you greater clarity today?
2. How can you strengthen your focus to support your goals?

CORNERSTONE TRUTHS

1. The mind is the architect
   of reality—thoughts
   shape destiny.
2. Mastery of the mind
   requires reframing, focus,
   and intentional design.
3. Neglected, the mind builds prisons; mastered, it
   builds palaces.

REFLECTION QUESTIONS

1. What limiting beliefs are currently shaping your
   reality?
2. How could you reframe a recent challenge into
   an empowering meaning?
3. What daily practice could help you polish the
   lens of your mind?

"Master your mind, and you master your world."

CHAPTER SEVEN

SPIRITUAL: CONNECTION TO PURPOSE AND TRANSCENDENCE

"You do not have a soul. You are a soul. You have a body."

— C.S. LEWIS

INCREDIBLY POWERFUL, UNSEEN FORCE

SPIRIT IS THE DIMENSION OF LIFE THAT ANCHORS everything else. It is the unseen force that gives meaning to action, depth to achievement, and resilience to suffering. You can strengthen the body, sharpen the mind, and even accumulate results, but without spirit, life feels empty—like a house with no foundation, a song with no melody.

Spirit is not confined to religion, though for some it flows through faith traditions. Spirit is your connection to purpose, to transcendence, to something greater than yourself. It is the awareness that you are more than flesh and thought, you are essence. When spirit is aligned, every area of life takes on clarity and weight. When it is neglected, even success feels hollow.

Why cultivate spirit? Because spirit answers the question of why. Why endure struggle? Why strive for greatness? Why love, forgive, or sacrifice? Spirit connects you to meaning beyond transaction. Why not? Because in the busyness of daily life, spirit feels intangible, secondary, or even optional. Many dismiss it until a crisis hits: illness, loss, or betrayal—when the absence of spirit suddenly becomes undeniable.

WHEN THE GRIND BECOMES YOUR GOD

In the trades industry, it's easy to let the grind replace your God. As soon as you wake up, you have to check the schedule, answer calls, call employees, call providers, call contractors, call clients, put out fires, chase invoices, deal with unexpected barriers, and come home exhausted. Then, it's rinse and repeat. The work can become all-consuming, and before you know it, Sunday morning becomes the day you catch up on paperwork instead of the day you go to church.

I've been there. I told myself I was building something for my family. It was worth every sacrifice, including my spiritual one. I was connecting with customers and creating jobs, which are good things, but that filled the void that used to be filled when I connected with God.

The business became my identity. I wasn't Steven Addario – believer, husband, father, son – I was Steven Addario – Owner of a Plumping and HVAC company.

I got a well-deserved slap in the face wake-up call when my son asked me to play catch. I said, "Not now, buddy, Dad's got to finish this estimate." He didn't ask again that week or the following. I played it over in my head and wondered what I had just taught him: that Dad was doing this for him or that Dad prioritized work over him, again?

The realization of how many times I must have done something similar to that gutted me. I can't properly express how much I love my wife and each of my kids. But I had let the trades consume me. The work never stops. There are always competitors. It's a dog-eat-dog world. You eat what you kill. To the victors go the spoils. There was always another call, another emergency, another opportunity – but I have one soul, one eternity, and one family. I told myself that I had to be better, and I think I have, at least I try to be, every single day. What use is it if I gain every material possession in this world, but lose my spirit?

SPIRIT

Spirit is like the roots of a tree. Invisible beneath the soil, but they hold everything upright. Cut the roots, and the tree withers no matter how green the leaves look for a time. Nourish the roots, and the tree flourishes.

Spirit is also like a compass. You may be running fast in life, but without a compass you may be heading in the wrong direction. Purpose provides true north. Spirit is that compass, it orients your actions toward meaning.

Finally, spirit is like fire in a hearth. It provides warmth and light to all who gather around. A house may be beautiful, but without fire it feels cold and empty. Spirit is the flame of life.

Consider Jesus in the wilderness. For forty days He fasted, prayed, and confronted temptation. His power didn't come from physical strength or social position; it came from spiritual alignment. His spirit remained unbreakable, even when tested by hunger, isolation, and attack.

Or look at Jesus washing the feet of His disciples. The King of Kings chose the posture of a servant. His spirit transformed service into greatness, proving that humility fueled by love can carry more authority than any crown.

And then there is Jesus on the cross. His body broken, His voice strained, yet His spirit radiated forgiveness: *"Father, forgive them, for they know not what they do."* That transcendent spirit not only endured suffering but transformed it into the greatest symbol of redemption in human history.

A parent who sacrifices sleep to care for a child does so not just out of duty but out of spiritual connection, love that transcends comfort. An artist pouring their soul into a painting taps into spirit, giving life to color and form.

In NLP, the spirit connects through values. When you live aligned with your highest values, you feel congruent and whole. When you violate them, inner conflict tears at you. Clarifying values, family, service, freedom, growth, guides spiritual integrity.

Anchoring transcendence is possible. Recall a moment of awe, standing at the edge of the ocean, holding your newborn child, or praying deeply. By anchoring that state to a gesture, word, or breath, you can reconnect to spirit anytime, anywhere.

Timeline work in NLP also integrates spirit. By envisioning your future self-fulfilled, and then stepping into that image, you pull spiritual purpose from the future into the present.

What if you ignored your spirit? Success might fill your bank account but leave you empty inside. Relationships might exist but lack depth. Achievements might come but feel meaningless. What if, instead, you nurtured your spirit daily? Every act could become infused with purpose. Ordinary days would shine with extraordinary meaning.

What if you measured your life not only by accomplishments but by alignment with purpose? How differently would you spend your days if spirit was the scorecard?

Martin Luther King Jr. drew spiritual strength from his faith, which infused his leadership with courage and compassion. His speeches still stir souls because they came from spirit, not just intellect.

Helen Keller Though deaf and blind, Keller's life radiated light. She believed spirit could transcend every physical limitation. Her writings and speeches were infused with hope and a deep sense of spiritual connection, proving that the human spirit can illuminate even the darkest realities.

There was a season when everything felt heavier than I could carry. Business stress piled on, family responsibilities pressed in, and I found myself staring at the ceiling at 2 a.m., wondering how much longer I could keep going. It felt like being in a tunnel with no light at the end.

What carried me through wasn't strategy or willpower. It was spiritual connection. Every morning, before my feet touched the ground, I made space to pray. Sometimes it wasn't eloquent, just a whispered, *"God, help me."* I opened scripture, even if it was just a single verse, and let those words anchor me when nothing else made sense.

There were moments when I felt something bigger than me step in, a calm that didn't come from me, a sense of direction when I had none, an assurance that I wasn't alone. That connection didn't erase the challenges, but it gave me the strength to walk through them without breaking.

"When your strength runs out, spirit carries you further."

Not all spiritual moments come in crisis. Some come in the most ordinary, beautiful places.

I remember standing at the edge of our new place, Legacy Estates, one summer evening with my family. The kids were laughing, the water was glass, and the sky lit up in colors no artist could ever capture. For a moment, time stopped. My worries, my plans, my to-do list, they all fell away. What filled me instead was awe.

In that moment, I felt transcendent. Larger than myself, yet more connected than ever. I wasn't just a man running a business or playing the role of husband and father. I was part of something vast, divine, woven into a story bigger than my own.

That sense of spirit expanded me. It reminded me that success without connection is empty, but when you anchor yourself in something greater, even the ordinary becomes sacred.

"Spirit turns ordinary moments into sacred ones."

Think of life as an instrument. The body is the instrument itself—the wood and strings. The mind is the musician's technique. But spirit is the music. Without spirit, there may be noise, but no song. With spirit, life becomes a symphony.

Here's an NLP-inspired spiritual practice you can adopt:

1. Each morning, anchor into gratitude by recalling three moments that lift your soul.
2. Visualize your day infused with purpose, seeing yourself acting with love and clarity.
3. Align decisions with values by asking: Does this serve my highest purpose?
4. Use breath or gesture anchors to return to presence when stressed.
5. End the day by connecting to meaning—reflect on who you served, what you created, and what you learned.

What if spirit guided all seven life areas?

- In health: you'd see your body as sacred, caring for it as a gift.
- In wealth: money would become a tool for service, not just accumulation.

- In relationships: love would be unconditional and expansive.
- In vocation: work would align with calling, not just paycheck.
- In spirit itself: practices would anchor you daily.
- In social impact: contribution would flow naturally.
- In mindset: peace would replace anxiety as you trust a higher design.

Picture yourself years from now, living in full spiritual alignment. You wake each day with clarity of purpose, moving through challenges with peace and power. Your presence uplifts others not because of what you do, but because of who you are. This is the fruit of nurturing spirit daily.

Now picture the opposite: success achieved but emptiness gnawing. Achievements without meaning. Recognition without fulfillment. This is the cost of neglecting spirit, the hollow echo of life without purpose.

Here's the reality nobody likes to talk or think about, but that everyone needs to face: one day, you're going to die. The business will close or go to someone else. The trucks will be sold. The bank account will be divided. Everything you spent your life building will go to someone else, and if you're lucky, it's your spouse and children, but sadly, that's not always the case for those who let work take precedence over their families.

Strip it all away, and what's left? Your spirit. Your soul. The results of what you've allowed yourself to think and do. The person you became. If you lived a good life, you leave behind many lives you've touched and the love you gave away without asking for anything in return.

It is my belief that I'll stand before the Big Guy one day. He's not going to ask me how big Addario's Services was or how much revenue we made. He isn't even going to ask me how much I tithed, because that promise is for the living, not when I'm in front of him. He's going to ask if I thought I served faithfully. But ultimately, the only question that matters is – did you use what I gave you to bring light into dark places?

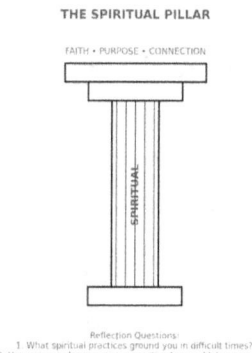

THE SPIRITUAL PILLAR

FAITH · PURPOSE · CONNECTION

SPIRITUAL

Reflection Questions:
1. What spiritual practices ground you in difficult times?
2. How can you deepen your connection to your higher purpose?

I'm writing this here, now, because I want to answer – yes, I tried. So go ahead, dear reader, build your business. Make your money. Take care of your family and loved ones. But never forget: the only thing you take with you when you leave is your spirit. Make sure you're building something eternal, not just something temporary.

CORNERSTONE TRUTHS

1. Spirit is the root system of life—it anchors and sustains everything else.
2. Spirit provides meaning, resilience, and transcendence.
3. Ignored, spirit leaves success hollow; nurtured, it makes life luminous.

REFLECTION QUESTIONS

1. What practices currently nourish your spirit, and how can you deepen them?
2. Where are you ignoring your spirit in pursuit of external results?
3. How might aligning with purpose transform your daily actions?

"Spirit is the fire that makes life luminous—without it, even the brightest achievements fade."

CHAPTER EIGHT

FAMILIAL: THE CORE OF CONNECTION AND LEGACY

"In every conceivable manner, the family is link to our past, bridge to our future."

— ALEX HALEY

ARE YOU REALLY SUCCESSFUL?

I'M NO HATER. I ADMIRE PEOPLE WHO HAVE BECOME VERY successful. I've even paid for some of them to coach me, a move that has paid off in droves. However, not everyone who is monetarily successful is someone I would say is winning at life. The road to success has crushed many families. The fame and authority must feel hollow to lose your family to success. Even worse is losing your family in pursuit of success, only to not even become successful!

Someone who has ruined relationships with their parents, wives, husband, children, siblings, and cherished, dear friends in pursuit of success is a sad creature. It's like going to the very best restaurant, every day, but having no one to share it with, no one you care about to roll your eyes with at how delicious the food is. I think of it like this: if you can't share it with your loved ones, how much of it can you really enjoy?

THE EMERGENCY CALL VS. THE DINNER TABLE

In the trades, the family tension is constant and real. The boiler doesn't care if you're having dinner with your family. It doesn't care that it's your mother's 90th birthday dinner. When you're in Massachusetts, and it's a freezing cold early evening during the month of February, and the boiler or heater stops working, your clients, who are freezing in their home, also don't care.

The family is having a great time, and the phone rings. Your wife gives you the look that says, 'don't pick it up. Let's enjoy this time. Call back after dinner.' Yet, you promised your clients that your service is unmatched in the area, so you pick up the phone.

"Steven, I'm so glad you picked up the phone. I have a serious emergency!"

Five minutes later, you're in a freezing cold truck, calling an employee to also leave his family to help you save the client and his family who are wearing boots, coats, hats, and gloves in their living room. This is the battle every good trade business owner faces, especially when you're building up the business. Do you not go? Do you let the customer fire you and tell everyone he knows how you let him and his family freeze for two days? No. You go. The work never stops. Weekends aren't sacred – sometimes they're peak calling time for emergencies!

For years, I convinced myself that I do this for them. I looked them in the eye and repeated it over and over, hoping that the saying is true – repetition works. I said it because there was some truth in that, but it was also a convenient excuse, if I'm being honest. I wanted success.

For some people, hiding in their work is easier than being present at home. At work, they have control. They could fix things. They're the experts. They're the hero who saves the day. At home? Temper tantrums. Unfixable. Wife with emotional issues. Unreachable. Teenagers who didn't even know they weren't home because they were with their friends or locked in their rooms playing video games. Unseen. Some people beg for calls to take them out of their homes.

The trades business, like many others, gives you a built-in escape hatch from family. Some people fake the calls to get out of their houses. They have no idea the danger they're putting themselves into. If they're not careful, they'll use that escape hatch so often that when they finally want to come home, they find that their family has learned to live without them.

FAMILY

Family is the heartbeat of life. It is where we first learn love, trust, and belonging. It is the classroom of values, the anchor of identity, and the soil in which our legacy grows. You can achieve riches, fame, and recognition, but without family, whether biological, chosen, or spiritual, there is an emptiness that no accolade can fill.

Family is more than blood. It is the network of people who know you deeply, who celebrate your triumphs, and walk with you through trials. It is where the human need for connection is met most intimately. Strong families build strong individuals, and strong individuals build strong societies.

Why prioritize family? Because love and connection sustain us in ways that money and achievements never can. Family provides grounding when the world shakes, perspective when pride inflates, and comfort when loss arrives. Why not? Because family relationships are often messy, complex, and demanding. It is easier to avoid conflict than to address it. Many pursue external success while neglecting family, only to discover later that hollow victories cannot replace broken bonds.

Family is like the root system of a tree. Hidden beneath the soil, roots nourish and stabilize. Cut off from roots, even the tallest tree eventually falls. Strong roots support growth that reaches to the sky.

Family is also like the hearth in a home. It provides warmth, light, and a place to gather. A house without a hearth may have walls, but it lacks heart. Family is the hearth of life.

Finally, family is like a foundation stone. Without it, the structure of life is fragile. You may build tall towers of success, but without family, the foundation cracks under pressure.

Consider the Kennedy family. Beyond politics, their strength came from shared rituals, meals, and traditions that bound them together. The legacy of leadership was nurtured at the family table long before it reached the world stage.

Or think of Nelson Mandela. Despite decades in prison, his connection to family anchored him. He drew strength from the vision of reconciliation not just for a nation but for his own family relationships.

In business, many founders who endured challenges credit their families as the reason they persevered. Howard Schultz of Starbucks often recalls the pain of watching his father struggle without support. That memory drove him to build a company that treated employees like family.

On the other hand, history is filled with stories of people who gained the world but lost their families. Many CEOs, celebrities, and leaders later confessed that their greatest regret was neglecting family in the pursuit of success. Broken marriages, estranged children, and lonely old age remind us that without family, achievement rings hollow.

In NLP, family relationships thrive when communication is intentional. Anchoring love through rituals, like shared meals or family traditions, creates states of connection. Reframing conflict turns battles into opportunities for understanding. Modeling communication patterns, listening deeply, validating feelings, pacing before leading, creates harmony.

For example, when a child acts out, reframing the behavior as a request for attention shifts the response from punishment to connection. When spouses argue, recognizing meta-programs (one seeks big picture, the other details) can prevent misunderstanding.

What if you treated family as your greatest investment? Imagine spending as much intentional time with your loved ones as you do on your business. What if every holiday, every dinner, every bedtime story was seen as legacy-building? How different would your children's lives be?

What if you neglected family? You might build wealth but die with regret. You might achieve influence but feel isolated at the top. What if, instead, you wove family into your definition of success? You would not only build empires but also raise heirs prepared to steward them.

Think of a grandparent who tells stories to their grandchildren. Those stories outlive the teller, passing values through generations. Or a parent who chooses to attend the school play instead of another meeting. That one act of presence becomes a lifelong memory for the child.

There were seasons in business where the weight felt unbearable, payroll looming, trucks breaking down, phone calls that brought more problems than solutions. In those moments, what kept me standing wasn't money or momentum. It was family.

I'd walk through the door at night, drained and discouraged, only to be greeted by my kids running to hug me, my wife smiling even though she carried her own load. That simple act, being reminded that I wasn't just a business owner but a father and husband, gave me resilience I couldn't have manufactured on my own. Their love wasn't conditional on whether I had a good day at work. It was steady. That steadiness gave me the courage to go back out and fight another round.

"Family doesn't erase the fight. It gives you strength to keep fighting."

THE UNSUNG HERO(INE)

Let me address something that doesn't get talked about enough. I've read books about trades. I've been to countless conferences, seminars, Zoom calls, masterminds, and meetings, and I rarely hear what I'm about to say to you. This could be true for every business owner, but I know it is definitely true for the trades business owner – the wife carries a weight most people never see.

She's the one who explains to the kids why Daddy missed another game. She reminds them that their dad loves them so much that he's working extremely hard to give them better opportunities than he had. She's the one managing the household, dealing with tantrums, staying on top of the kids for doing their homework, doing the laundry, cooking, cleaning, taking the kids to school or their sports or their part-time jobs, organizing play dates, and explains to your mother when it's her 90th birthday, that you had to leave but that you love her very much.

She answers your phone at 9 PM and saves you from flying out the door so you can get a good night's rest. She's the one who listens to you vent about employees, customers, and cash flow, while her own stresses go unspoken to you because she knows you're maxed out.

The part that breaks my heart, but I'm thankful that I was coachable and changed my ways, is that for too many years, I took my wife, Maria, for granted. I thought that because she knew I was a hard-working man, doing everything I could to provide, was enough. I thought bringing home big paychecks was all I needed to do to show up as a good husband.

It's not.

Yes, Maria wanted financial security, we all do – but not more than a partner. She didn't need me to be perfect, or to have the largest HVAC company in my area – she needed me to be present. She didn't need me to fix everything – she needed me to listen to her when she needed it, to see her, and to acknowledge that her work keeping our children safe, spiritually grounded, and loved was just as valuable, if not more, than my working on building the business.

One of the greatest gifts I've discovered is how much meaning lives in the small family rituals. Whether it's dinners around the table, holiday traditions, or Sunday routines, those little moments become anchors for identity.

For my kids, it wasn't the big vacations or the fancy gifts that mattered most. It was the predictability of certain traditions, the way we showed up together, laughed together, and carved out sacred space in the chaos of life. Even today, I can see how those rituals built a sense of stability and belonging in them. And in me.

Those moments remind me that family legacy isn't built in occasional fireworks. It's built with steady candles that keep burning year after year.

"Traditions are the threads that weave family into legacy."

But I'd be lying if I said I always got it right. There were times I let ambition run ahead of family. I told myself I was working for them, while in reality, I was working *away* from them. Missed dinners. Missed games. Missed moments I can't ever buy back.

The lesson came the hard way, seeing the look in my wife's eyes when I was physically present but mentally absent. Hearing my kids ask, "Are you coming this time?" That cut deeper than any business setback ever could.

It forced me to recalibrate. To realize that success in the world means nothing if it costs you success at home. I shifted my priorities, protecting family time, building rhythms that honored them as much as my work, and remembering that the business exists to serve the family, not the other way around.

"If you win the world and lose your family, you've lost."

POWERFUL FAMILY BONDS

Family is like a tapestry. Each person is a thread. Alone, a thread can fray. Together, woven with intention, threads create a picture of beauty and strength. Remove threads, and holes appear. Strengthen the weave, and the tapestry lasts for generations.

Here's an NLP-inspired framework to strengthen family bonds:

1. Anchor family connection to consistent rituals—meals, game nights, weekly check-ins.
2. Reframe conflicts as opportunities for growth—ask, 'What value is being expressed here?'
3. Model the communication you wish to see—calm, validating, respectful.
4. Use language patterns of appreciation daily—catch loved ones doing things right.
5. Visualize family flourishing—see generations connected, strong, and united.

What if family harmony influenced all seven life areas?

- In health: family support encourages good habits.
- In wealth: family unity preserves generational assets.
- In relationships: family models shape all future connections.
- In vocation: family gives purpose to hard work.
- In spirit: family traditions anchor transcendence.
- In social impact: strong families model strong societies.
- In mindset: family belonging creates resilience and confidence.

Picture yourself decades from now, surrounded by children and grandchildren. They look to you with gratitude, not because of what you built alone, but because of the family you nurtured. Picture your legacy not just in dollars but in stories, traditions, and love passed down. This is the fruit of prioritizing family.

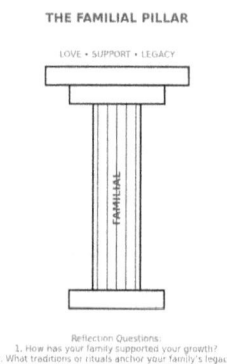

THE FAMILIAL PILLAR

LOVE · SUPPORT · LEGACY

FAMILIAL

Reflection Questions:
1. How has your family supported your growth?
2. What traditions or rituals anchor your family's legacy?

Now picture the opposite: wealth accumulated but family estranged. A funeral attended by colleagues but not children. This is the cost of neglect. The choice is daily—neglect or nurture, disconnection or connection.

CORNERSTONE TRUTHS

1. Family is the root system of life—it grounds and nourishes everything.
2. Neglect of family makes success hollow; nurturing family multiplies legacy.
3. Family is built in daily rituals, presence, and intentional love.

REFLECTION QUESTIONS

1. Where are you prioritizing external success over family connection?
2. What rituals could you create to strengthen your family bonds?
3. How would redefining success to include family change your daily choices?

"Family is the hearth of life—neglect it and the fire dies, nurture it and the flame lights generations."

CHAPTER NINE

SOCIAL: THE POWER OF CONNECTION BEYOND FAMILY

"The quality of your life is the quality of your relationships."

— TONY ROBBINS

RELATIONSHIPS ARE THE BRIDGES THAT CARRY US ACROSS the landscapes of life. Family may be our roots, but relationships beyond family, friendships, partnerships, mentorships, communities, become the branches that expand our reach. They open doors we cannot open alone, provide mirrors that reflect our blind spots, and offer support that multiplies our potential.

No one achieves greatness in isolation. Every visionary had allies, every innovator had collaborators, every leader had followers. The myth of the self-made person dissolves under scrutiny, our lives are interwoven with others. Relationships are not optional, they are essential.

Why prioritize relationships? Because they expand perspective, multiply resources, and provide emotional nourishment. Strong relationships accelerate growth, magnify joy, and buffer hardship. Why not? Because relationships are risky. They demand vulnerability, patience, and compromise. They expose us to betrayal, disappointment, and hurt. Yet the risk of pain is far outweighed by the cost of isolation.

Relationships are like gardens. Left untended, they wither. With care, they blossom. They require planting seeds of trust, watering with time, and pruning through honest communication.

They are also like mirrors. They reflect truths we cannot see alone, our strengths, flaws, and blind spots. Avoiding relationships means avoiding the mirrors that help us grow.

Finally, relationships are like bridges. They connect us to opportunities, ideas, and experiences across divides we could never cross alone.

Orville and Wilbur Wright weren't just inventors; they were brothers who sharpened each other's genius. One had the mechanical vision; the other had the practical refinement. Their shared obsession, collaboration, and constant exchange of ideas lifted humanity off the ground — literally. Their social bond gave wings to invention

Think of the partnership between Steve Jobs and Steve Wozniak. One was visionary, the other a technical genius. Together they built Apple. Separately, their potential may have remained dormant. Their relationship created synergy greater than the sum of their parts.

Mentorship also changes destinies. Socrates mentored Plato, who mentored Aristotle, who mentored Alexander the Great. One relationship rippled across history, shaping philosophy, science, and leadership.

But relationships mishandled can destroy. Julius Caesar trusted Brutus and paid with his life. Business partnerships fractured by ego have collapsed companies. Friendships neglected have withered into estrangement. The power of relationships cuts both ways, they can elevate or devastate.

In NLP, building rapport is the foundation of powerful relationships. Matching and mirroring posture, tone, and pace creates unconscious alignment. People feel understood, and trust grows. Once rapport is established, pacing and leading allows you to guide interaction toward greater outcomes.

Reframing conflict transforms arguments into opportunities. Instead of seeing disagreement as opposition, it can be reframed as diversity of perspective. Anchoring positive states—such as laughter or shared victories, strengthens bonds, making it easier to weather storms.

Think of two friends who commit to exercising together. The accountability and camaraderie multiply results. Or a mastermind group of entrepreneurs who challenge and support each other, each member rising higher than they could alone.

Even casual relationships, a kind neighbor, a supportive colleague, can shift life trajectories. Connection creates pathways for possibility.

What if you invested in relationships as intentionally as in business or fitness? What if you scheduled time for friends as seriously as meetings? Imagine the resilience built when you know you are never alone in hardship, and the joy multiplied when victories are shared.

What if you ignored relationships? Isolation corrodes. Success achieved in solitude feels empty. What if you climbed the ladder of success but found no one waiting at the top? Relationships determine whether success tastes sweet or bitter.

Along in my career, I thought success was a solo climb. Head down, work harder than everyone else, and the results would speak for themselves. But then I crossed paths with a mentor who saw something in me I didn't fully see in myself.

He didn't just give advice, he believed in me. And that belief shifted everything. When I hesitated, he challenged me. When I doubted, he reminded me of my potential. His influence expanded the size of the game I thought I could play. Suddenly, the goals that once felt out of reach became possible, because someone outside of my family spoke into me with conviction.

That relationship taught me a lesson I carry to this day: the right person in your corner can fast-forward your growth by years.

"One believer in your corner can multiply your vision tenfold."

Not all relationships end in growth. Some end in heartbreak, and the lessons last just as long.

There was a friendship I once invested deeply in. We built things together, celebrated wins together, trusted each other like brothers. But somewhere along the way, miscommunication, pride, and misaligned priorities crept in. Conversations turned sharp, trust eroded, and before long the relationship cracked.

Losing that friendship was one of the hardest hits I've taken, because it wasn't about business, it was personal. It forced me to confront how easily assumptions can harden into walls, and how silence can do more damage than conflict ever could.

The lesson was painful but priceless: relationships are fragile if you don't protect them with honesty, communication, and boundaries. Today, I approach my social circle with more intentionality. I'd rather have fewer deep connections built on truth than many shallow ones built on convenience. Had that relationship not ended like it did I would probably not be coaching or even writing this book. It took me a solid year to see that it was happening for me not to me. It had to happen for me to take the stage.

"Relationships die not from distance but from neglect."

Life is like an orchestra. Each relationship is an instrument. Alone, each makes sound; together, they make symphony. Neglect one, and the music falters. Nurture all, and the harmony inspires generations.

Here's an NLP-based practice for strengthening relationships:

1. Begin with rapport—notice breathing, tone, and posture, and align with it.
2. Listen actively—repeat back key words to show understanding.
3. Reframe disagreements by asking: 'What value are they expressing beneath this conflict?'
4. Anchor positive states by creating rituals of joy, shared meals, celebrations, traditions.
5. Visualize the relationship flourishing, imagine conversations filled with trust, laughter, and support.

The Wright brothers illustrate how sibling partnership fueled innovation. Each trusted the other completely, sharing failures and breakthroughs. Together, they built the first airplane and changed human history.

Modern entrepreneurs often credit networks of peers for their success. Mark Zuckerberg's creation of Facebook was catalyzed by relationships with fellow students, investors, and mentors. Without those relational bridges, the platform may never have scaled.

What if relationships amplified all seven life areas?

- In health: friends who share workouts keep you consistent.
- In wealth: partnerships open opportunities you could not reach alone.
- In relationships: friendships teach you empathy beyond family.
- In vocation: mentors accelerate growth and skill.
- In spirit: shared practices deepen transcendence.
- In social impact: networks multiply influence.
- In mindset: supportive peers reinforce empowering beliefs.

Picture yourself ten years from now, surrounded not just by family but by a network of friendships and partnerships that uplift you. Imagine challenges faced with allies, victories celebrated in community, and a legacy of connection that outlives you.

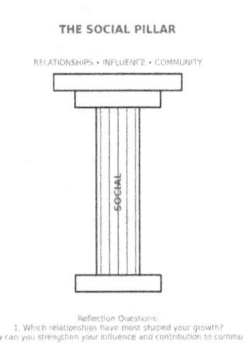

THE SOCIAL PILLAR

RELATIONSHIPS • INFLUENCE • COMMUNITY

SOCIAL

Reflection Questions:
1. Which relationships have most shaped your growth?
2. How can you strengthen your influence and contribution to community?

Now picture the opposite: success pursued in isolation, relationships neglected or abandoned. The mansion is built, but the rooms are empty. The victories are won, but no one is there to share them. This is the cost of neglecting relationships—the hollow echo of solitude.

CORNERSTONE TRUTHS

1. Relationships are bridges to growth, opportunity, and fulfillment.
2. Healthy relationships require investment, vulnerability, and care.
3. Neglected relationships lead to isolation, but nurtured ones create legacy.

REFLECTION QUESTIONS

1. Who outside your family has shaped your life most, and how can you honor them?
2. Where are you neglecting relationships that could become sources of joy and growth?
3. What daily or weekly rituals could you establish to nurture key connections?

"Life's symphony is written in relationships—alone there is noise, together there is music."

CHAPTER TEN

VOCATIONAL: ALIGNING WORK WITH CALLING

"Choose a job you love, and you will never have to work a day in your life."

— CONFUCIUS

VOCATION IS MORE THAN A JOB, MORE THAN A PAYCHECK, and more than the tasks you complete between Monday and Friday. It is not simply what you do to pay the bills, it is what you are called to express through your gifts, talents, and values. When you are vocationally aligned, even hard work feels energizing. You may feel tired at the end of the day, but it is the fatigue of fulfillment, not the exhaustion of emptiness. When you are vocationally misaligned, each hour feels like a burden. Time drags, creativity withers, and purpose fades.

We often mistake a job for a vocation. A job provides income, but a vocation provides meaning. A job can be replaced by another, but a vocation cannot be ignored without deep cost. It is the whisper that keeps returning, the dream that refuses to die, the vision that feels bigger than yourself. True vocation is not about what you do, it is about who you are when you are doing it.

Most people work jobs their entire lives. Not everyone finds their vocation. Almost every employee works a job, but almost every good business owner has a vocation. Employees interview for a job, business owners invest their hard-earned money in their vocation.

Interestingly enough, the word vocation comes from the Latin word *vocare*, which means "to call." I believe everyone has a calling, and it's a waste of people's lives to waste it without at least looking for it. It's important to realize that work consumes a third of life. To misalign work with purpose is to waste irreplaceable years. When vocation aligns with calling, each hour becomes an investment in destiny rather than a withdrawal from the soul. Pursuing a true vocation requires courage. It demands stepping out of one's comfort zone, leaving behind security, and sometimes disappointing others' expectations. Fear whispers, *"safety is better than calling,'* but in the long run, safety without meaning becomes suffocation.

Vocation is like a river. When it flows within its channel, it moves powerfully and purposefully. When it is blocked or diverted, it stagnates or floods, causing damage. Your calling is the channel. Work aligned with calling flows. Misalignment in the workplace becomes a stagnant pool that breeds frustration.

It is also like a fire in a furnace. Contained and directed, fire warms homes and forges steel. Misused or neglected, it either burns out of control or dies. Your work, like fire, must be channeled toward purpose if it is to generate true power.

Finally, vocation is like a compass. You may walk fast, even run, but if the compass is not set to true north, your speed leads you nowhere. The compass of vocation ensures that effort leads to destiny, not to dead ends.

Consider Miyamoto Musashi, who defied a life of wandering violence to pursue a higher vocation: mastery. His path was not merely about winning duels, though he won more than sixty without defeat. His true vocation was the lifelong pursuit of "The Way," a discipline that fused art, philosophy, and strategy. He trained relentlessly, wrote *The Book of Five Rings*, and taught that vocation is not a job but a calling, something that sustains you through exhaustion, isolation, and resistance. Musashi's life reminds us that true vocation is not about prestige; it is about aligning with a path so deeply that every step, every battle, every creation becomes an expression of purpose.

Leonardo da Vinci embodied vocational alignment. His curiosity spanned art, science, and engineering. His vocation was not one career, but the pursuit of discovery itself. His legacy is proof that vocation is about alignment with essence, not job titles.

Edison spent years chasing the light bulb, testing filament after filament. Bamboo, cotton thread, horsehair, even beards — he tried them all. Thousands of experiments ended in smoke, shatter, or short-lived sparks. Each "failure" drained money, tested patience, and drew ridicule from critics who said he was chasing the impossible.

What kept him going? Vocation. Edison wasn't tinkering for curiosity alone, he was called to bring light to the world. His own words echo his spirit: *"I have not failed. I've just found 10,000 ways that won't work."*

Those thousands of failed attempts became the steppingstones to one enduring success. And that's what vocation does: it transforms failure from a reason to quit into proof that you are still on the path. Edison's persistence wasn't stubbornness, it was alignment. When your work is a vocation, resistance doesn't defeat you; it refines you.

Modern examples abound. Oprah Winfrey aligned her vocation with her ability to connect, empathize, and communicate. Her work as a talk show host was not just a job, it was her calling expressed at scale. Elon Musk channels his audacity into innovations in space and energy, expressing his calling to push humanity forward.

On the other hand, millions remain stuck in jobs that suffocate their souls. They live for weekends, dreading Mondays. Imagine going your entire life dreading Mondays, which always come. It's a sad existence, my friend. Their talents remain buried, their creativity silenced. At retirement, they look back not with gratitude but with regret, wondering what might have been. This is the price of ignoring vocation, the silent erosion of life energy.

But people are so afraid of what others might think, they'll play small their entire lives. They think being called 'Ambitious' is a bad thing. They've been indoctrinated by poor people that going after their dreams is a form of being selfish. They've never followed their dreams, so they inadvertently or deliberately try to keep their family and friends from pursuing theirs.

I'm here to Hulk Smash that way of thinking: PLAYING SMALL IS THE MOST SELFISH THING YOU CAN DO!

When you stay small because you only play small, you're robbing yourself from your best life, you're never finding out what you're capable of, and you're not just hurting yourself – you're hurting your family. You come home with an angst that you're not doing enough, that your supervisor doesn't give you more to do, you're not making the money you'd like, and you spill that anger/anxiety/feeling of helplessness into alcohol, drugs, food, or you take it out on your spouse and kids. But the reality is, you hurt more than just your family.

You're robbing everyone who needed what only you could give. You've robbed new employees of the opportunity to work for a great boss. You've robbed the world of your talent. It's almost as if you never really lived.

- There are people who need the business you're afraid to start or afraid to grow.
- There are employees who need the jobs you're too scared to create.
- There are customers who need the problem solved, and only your unique combination of skills, experience, and perspective can solve it.

It's not easy. I get it. But know that every great innovator, leader, and creator had to overcome the temptation to play it safe. But imagine if the Wright Brothers stayed in the bicycle shop? Imagine if Edison had quit after the 100th failed attempt. Imagine if Martin Luther King Jr. had remained a comfortable pastor instead of risking his life to lead a movement.

Here's a question that I hope haunts you: What contribution are you withholding from the world by playing small? What problems are you allowing people to go through because you're afraid to step into your calling, or because you're afraid to go all out? The world doesn't need the you that plays small, it needs you – the real you, the full you, fully alive, fully expressed, and fully aligned with what you were put on this Earth to do.

In NLP, aligning vocation begins with eliciting values. Ask yourself: 'What is important to me about work?'

The answers reveal whether you value freedom, creativity, service, growth, or security. When work fulfills these values, energy flows. When work violates them, resistance builds.

Reframing also transforms the work experience. A repetitive task reframed as service to others becomes a contribution rather than drudgery. Anchoring passion into daily rituals, through music, visualization, or empowering affirmations, shifts the emotional state before entering work. Even within the same job, reframing can transform suffering into service, burnout into building.

At this very moment, as you read this, your inner voice might say, "This all sounds great, Steven, but I don't know what my calling is! How do I figure it out?"

Fair question. Here are three questions to answer. Draw three overlapping circles and label them as such:

1. What am I naturally good at? (Your gifts and talents)
2. What do I care deeply about? (Your passion and values)
3. What does the world need (What problems matter that you can solve)

Your vocation lives in the intersection of all three. It's a lot more than what you're good at, some people are good at things they hate or are sick of doing. It's not just about what you care about – passion without skill leads to frustration. It's also not just about what the world needs – duty without joy leads to burnout.

Your calling is where your gifts meet your passion and serve a real need.

Another NLP application is future pacing. Imagine stepping into your ideal vocational future. See it, hear it, feel it. By creating that sensory-rich image, you condition your nervous system to pursue it with clarity and conviction.

Consider the teacher who inspires children daily, the mechanic who treats every repair as service, or the barista who makes coffee with a smile. These vocations may seem ordinary, but when aligned with calling, they ripple extraordinary meaning into the lives of others.

Or the entrepreneur who risks comfort to start a business aligned with passion. The long hours no longer feel like punishment, they feel like purpose. Alignment transforms effort into enthusiasm.

What if you fully aligned your vocation with your calling? Mornings would begin with energy rather than dread. Even challenges would feel purposeful, because they serve a bigger vision. Time would pass quickly, creativity would flow, and contribution would multiply. You'd come to the house ready to play, not to fight.

What if you ignored your calling for another decade? Imagine the regrets. Dreams unpursued, talents buried, impact lost. The pain of discipline is small compared to the pain of regret. Being called out becomes a wound that never fully heals.

I know people who have complained to me that they don't make enough money to take good vacations every year. Yet, five years pass, and they're still at the same job, giving the same complaints. I don't get it. You can learn almost anything on YouTube.

In the book, The Fierce Urgency of Now, author Eli Gonzalez dedicated an entire chapter called 45 is 45. The premise is that everyone has 45 minutes a day to devote to something new, whether it's learning guitar, becoming a better cook, mastering AI, or pursuing a profession. Regardless, you're going to live through those 45 minutes. You can stack those 45 minutes a day and change your life, or you can play video games in your free time. Whatever you do with your free 45 minutes can determine your future.

I was only twenty-one when I started my business. No roadmap. No investors. Just a truck, some tools, and the willingness to outwork anyone. At the time, I didn't think of it as a "calling." It felt more like survival. But as the years went on, I realized I wasn't just fixing plumbing or HVAC systems, I was building something that mattered.

The obstacles were brutal. Sleepless nights, financial setbacks, and the constant pressure of being the one everyone looked to for answers. There were moments I thought about quitting, when the weight of responsibility felt crushing. But every time I got knocked down, something deeper pulled me back up: the sense that this was what I was made to do. My vocation wasn't a job. It was the arena where I discovered who I truly was.

"Calling isn't found in comfort. It's discovered in the obstacles you refuse to surrender to."

But there was also a season where I drifted. I got caught up in chasing money, growth for the sake of growth, and the next big win. On the surface, everything looked good, the trucks were rolling, the jobs were booked, the numbers kept climbing. But inside, I was empty. I wasn't leading from calling anymore. I was grinding from ego.

The cost was heavy. I felt disconnected from the very thing that had once given me purpose. The passion dimmed, my patience wore thin, and I found myself wondering if it was all worth it.

The realignment came when I slowed down enough to remember *why* I started. My vocation wasn't about stacking dollars. It was about serving people, creating opportunities, and leaving a legacy. When I re-centered on that truth, everything shifted. The fire came back. The business grew again, this time on the solid ground of purpose instead of the shaky ground of pride.

"Ignore your vocation and you lose yourself. Rediscover it and you come alive again."

One of the greatest rewards of living your calling is helping others discover theirs. I'll never forget mentoring a young guy by the name of Brian who came into the trades unsure of himself. He had raw talent but no direction. At first, he treated the work like just another paycheck. But I saw something in him.

Through coaching, accountability, and sometimes tough love, I pushed him to see the bigger picture, that his work could be a craft, a service, even a calling. Slowly, he caught it. His confidence grew, his skills sharpened, and he began to lead others.

Years later, he told me, "If you hadn't pushed me, I'd still be drifting." Now he's mentoring others, passing on the same belief I once gave him. That's the ripple effect of vocation, when your calling awakens someone else's, the legacy multiplies beyond what you can measure.

"The highest proof of calling is when it awakens calling in others."

Your vocation is like an instrument in the orchestra of humanity. Play it well, and the symphony of life is enriched. Ignore it, and the music is incomplete. Every vocation matters—yours is part of the greater harmony of existence.

Here's an NLP-based framework for aligning vocation:

1. Identify your top five values about work—freedom, security, growth, creativity, service.
2. Rank them. Notice which values your current work fulfills and which it violates.
3. Reframe daily tasks—connect them to contribution and growth.
4. Anchor passion—create a ritual before work that primes you emotionally.
5. Visualize your vocational future daily—step into it as if it already exists.
6. Take one action each week that moves you closer to alignment, no matter how small.

What if vocation alignment transformed all seven life areas?

- In health: meaningful work energizes rather than drains.
- In wealth: prosperity flows from passion and creativity.
- In relationships: vocational joy spills into family life.
- In vocation: dread turns into delight.
- In spirit: work becomes worship, a form of service.

- In social impact: your gifts contribute to community.
- In mindset: alignment produces confidence and resilience.

Picture yourself five years from now in vocational alignment. You wake up energized, contribute with passion, and end each day fulfilled. Your family thrives from your joy, your community grows from your service, and your legacy expands with each decision aligned with calling.

Now picture the opposite, five more years of misalignment. Each day drains energy, resentment grows, and creativity dies. The paycheck arrives, but joy does not. This is the cost of avoiding vocation, the slow death of potential.

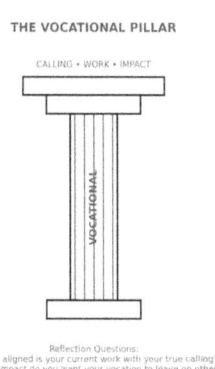

THE VOCATIONAL PILLAR

CALLING • WORK • IMPACT

VOCATIONAL

Reflection Questions:
1. How aligned is your current work with your true calling?
2. What impact do you want your vocation to leave on others?

CORNERSTONE TRUTHS

1. Vocation is calling expressed through contribution.
2. Alignment produces joy, energy, and legacy.
3. Misalignment drains life; alignment expands it.

REFLECTION QUESTIONS

1. What values matter most to you in work?
2. Where is your current work aligned or misaligned?
3. What small step could you take today toward vocational alignment?

"Vocation aligned with calling transforms labor into legacy."

CHAPTER ELEVEN

FINANCIAL: MASTERING MONEY AS A SERVANT, NOT A MASTER

"Do not save what is left after spending, but spend what is left after saving."

— WARREN BUFFETT

FINANCES ARE ONE OF THE MOST MISUNDERSTOOD AND emotionally charged areas of life. For some, money is a source of anxiety and fear. For others, it is an idol worshiped above health, family, and spirit. The truth is that money itself is neutral, it is a tool. When mastered, it serves as a servant, fueling freedom, impact, and legacy. When neglected or idolized, it becomes a master that enslaves.

Financial mastery is not about greed or hoarding. It is about alignment, bringing money into harmony with your values and purpose. Money can fund dreams, sustain families, build communities, and expand impact. But when unmanaged, it multiplies stress, breeds conflict, and limits freedom. Like fire, money warms when controlled, but burns when left untended.

Most people go through predictable stages in their financial journeys. Understanding where you are helps you see where you're going, and how to get there.

Stage 1 – Survival Mode: This is paycheck-to-paycheck living; we've all been there. Every end of the month is a scramble for the rent or mortgage. One unexpected expense – a car repair, a medical bill, or having to bail your great-grandmother out of jail – creates a crisis.

- If you're here, the goal is simple: Stop the Bleeding. Create a basic budget and adhere to it. It may take a little while but build a small emergency fund ($1,00-$2,000). Stop accumulating new debt. Stop living above your means. Stop going out to eat so often. Stop drinking so much. This stage is about getting your head above water.

Stage 2 – Stability: You're no longer drowning, but you're not thriving either. You can cover your bills, maybe even save a little. You can go to any restaurant whenever you'd like. However, one bad month could still knock you back to Stage 1 for months.

- If you're here, the goal is simple: Build Buffers. Save up a 3–6-month emergency fund. Pay off high-interest debt, get rid of them! Get intentional about where your money goes. Budgeting is no longer a hindrance, you start to get excited because you can start to see the next stage.

Stage 3 – Security: Now you're building wealth. Debt is manageable if not gone entirely. You're consistently saving, maybe even doing some investing. You can handle emergencies without panic.

- If you're here, the goal is simple: Shift from Defense to Offense. Maximize retirement contributions, invest in income-producing assets, build streams of passive income, and start thinking about legacy. This is where compounding becomes your best friend.

Stage 4: Significance: This is where everyone wants to be, even those who don't admit it. You have more than enough. Your needs are covered, your future is secure, your children and grandchildren's educations are paid for, and your big question is: what do I do with the rest of this wealth? Money becomes a tool for impact – generosity, philanthropy, and creating opportunities for others. You don't worry about how much you have, you lose sleep over how much to give and how to make your money help others.

- If you're here, the goal is simple: Teach others to get where you are. Invest in inspired dreamers. Help fight against diseases that have hurt you. Leave a legacy that outlives you.

Why pursue financial mastery? Because money touches every other area of life. Health requires resources. Family requires provision. Vocation flourishes with financial foundation. Spirit and contribution expand with resources. Finances are not everything, but without them, other pursuits are hindered. Why not? Because dealing with money can feel overwhelming. Many avoid budgets, investments, and planning because they fear failure or feel unqualified. They settle for survival instead of stewardship.

Finances are like water. Without it, life withers. With too much uncontrolled flow, it floods and destroys. Managed well, water nourishes growth. Money, like water, must be directed with wisdom.

Finances are like fuel. A car without fuel goes nowhere, no matter how powerful the engine. Fuel without direction, however, can explode. Money is fuel, without it, dreams stall; misused, it can destroy.

Finances are like a magnifying glass. They do not change who you are, they simply amplify it. In the hands of the wise, money magnifies generosity and growth. In the hands of the foolish, it magnifies recklessness and greed.

Consider Warren Buffett. Starting with small investments in his youth, he mastered patience and the power of compounding. His wealth was not built overnight but through decades of disciplined reinvestment. Today, his fortune is not just a monument to compounding, it is also a tool for philanthropy, as he pledges most of it to causes beyond himself.

Think of everyday families who consistently save and invest. By directing even modest sums into retirement accounts, college funds, or businesses, they build stability that ripples across generations. Wealth, when stewarded, creates freedom long after the earner is gone.

Contrast this with lottery winners who squander millions within years. Without stewardship, sudden wealth magnifies poor habits. Or celebrities who earn fortunes but end bankrupt because spending outpaced wisdom. Money without mastery destroys as quickly as it creates.

One of the most powerful forces in finance is compound interest. Albert Einstein is often credited with calling it 'the eighth wonder of the world.' Yet most people underestimate it. Why? Because compounding works slowly at first, almost invisibly. The early years seem insignificant. A hundred dollars invested grows to one hundred and ten, then one hundred and twenty-one. The change feels small, so people dismiss it. But given time, compounding becomes exponential.

Here's an example: If you invest $500 a month at a modest 8% annual return, in 10 years you will have about \$91,000. In 20 years, \$274,000. In 30 years, over \$745,000. The later years create the largest jumps because interest is earned not only on the original contributions but also on the accumulated interest. The final decade often produces more growth than the first two combined. Yet because people crave instant results, they miss the miracle of compounding.

Why is compounding overlooked? Because our brains are wired for linear thinking. We expect growth to be steady and slow. Exponential growth feels foreign. In finances, compounding hides its power in plain sight, demanding patience, discipline, and vision. In NLP terms, compounding is a reframing exercise in time perspective: shifting focus from immediate gratification to long-term abundance.

In NLP, money beliefs often determine financial destiny more than income does. If you believe 'money is scarce,' you unconsciously repel opportunities. If you believe 'money is a tool for good,' you attract and steward it. Reframing scarcity into stewardship transforms anxiety into empowerment.

Anchoring abundance can be practiced daily. Each time you make a wise financial choice, saving instead of spending, investing instead of consuming, anchor the feeling of empowerment. These conditions your nervous system to associate money with control and freedom rather than fear.

Collapsing limiting beliefs about money is also critical. If you were raised hearing 'money is the root of all evil,' replace it with 'the love of money is the root of all evil, but money itself is a magnifier.' This shift releases guilt and allows alignment between wealth and purpose.

A young couple who budgets consistently may never feel glamorous, but ten years later, they own their home debt-free. A business owner who reinvests profits into training and systems may not enjoy as much cash flow today, but five years later, their company doubles in size. Financial mastery is built not on dramatic wins but on daily disciplines.

Early in my career, I didn't fully understand the power of compounding. Like a lot of young business owners, I thought only big leaps made big differences. But one year, I made the decision to start setting aside a small percentage of every job that came in, no matter how tight things felt. It wasn't flashy. Some weeks it looked almost laughable. But I stuck with it.

Months turned into years, and what once felt like pocket change grew into something substantial. That little reservoir became the down payment for equipment, the cushion during slow seasons, and the safety net that kept us from taking on high-interest debt. The lesson hit me hard: the market doesn't reward size of effort alone, it rewards consistency over time.

That habit bled into my personal life too. Investing early, even in small amounts, taught me patience. The results didn't explode overnight, but one day I looked up and realized those little deposits had turned into something big enough to change my options.

"Wealth is rarely built in leaps. It's built in layers of small, faithful choices."

Of course, money has also taught me some painful lessons. There was a stretch where I chased growth so aggressively that I ignored financial discipline. I over-spent, over-leveraged, and assumed revenue would always outpace mistakes. For a while, it looked like it might. But the numbers don't lie.

The crash came when cash flow dried up, and I realized I had commitments I couldn't cover. That season was brutal. Sleepless nights, difficult conversations, and the shame of knowing I'd done it to myself. But as painful as it was, that mistake became the best financial coach I ever had.

I learned to track numbers obsessively, to build margins into every job, and to respect cash flow as the lifeblood of the business. That discipline changed everything. The very pain that once threatened to sink me became the foundation of financial abundance down the road.

"Mistakes with money are tuition. Pay once, learn forever."

Let me share with you what financial mastery actually gives you: OPTIONS.

When you're broke, you have no options. You can't even choose which color car you drive, you drive what you can afford and that's that. You take whatever job is offered because you need that check asap. You stay in the toxic relationship because you can't make it on your own. You can't help your parents when they need you. You can't pursue the business idea because you're trapped in survival mode. Every decision you make comes from the fear of scarcity, not abundance.

But when you master money? EVERYTHING CHANGES.

You can walk away from work where your boss demeans you and doesn't value you because you have 6 months of savings, more than enough time to find another good-paying job. You can take a risk on the business idea because if it doesn't work, the bills will still be paid, and the family will still eat well. You can be generous to your parents because you're not stressed about the bills. You can even say 'No' or a Stone Cold Steve Austin, 'Hell No' to opportunities that don't align with your calling because you're not desperate.

What if you ignored your finances? Bills pile up. Debt compounds in the wrong direction. Stress infiltrates health and relationships. What if, instead, you mastered money? Savings would grow. Investments would multiply. Freedom would expand. The difference between neglect and mastery is not income but intention.

Think of finances like a garden. Seeds planted today seem small, but years later, the harvest feeds generations. Neglect the garden, and weeds choke the soil. Overwater it, and rot sets in. Balance and patience yield abundance.

Or think of finances like fitness. No single workout transforms the body, but daily discipline over years sculpts strength. No single investment makes you rich, but consistent compounding builds wealth.

Here's an NLP-inspired framework for mastering money:

1. Identify your money beliefs. Write down three limiting ones and reframe them into empowering beliefs.
2. Anchor abundance. Each time you make a wise financial choice, create a physical anchor (like clenching your fist) to associate the decision with empowerment.
3. Reframe expenses. See them not as losses but as investments in health, family, vocation, or legacy.
4. Visualize long-term compounding. Picture your financial future ten, twenty, thirty years ahead.
5. Take one action each week—saving, investing, debt reduction—that builds momentum.

What if finances aligned with all seven life areas?

- In health: money funds preventive care and wellness.

- In family: money provides security and opportunity.
- In relationships: financial freedom reduces stress and increases joy.
- In vocation: money fuels passion projects and innovation.
- In spirit: money funds service and generosity.
- In social impact: wealth multiplies contribution.
- In mindset: financial mastery reduces anxiety and builds confidence.

Picture yourself twenty years from now. Because you mastered money, you have freedom. Your children are secure. Your community benefits from your generosity. You sleep in peace because money is no longer master but servant.

Now picture the opposite. Twenty years of neglect. Debt unpaid. Stress mounting. Opportunities missed. The regret is not only financial, it is emotional, relational, and spiritual. The choice is daily: mastery or neglect.

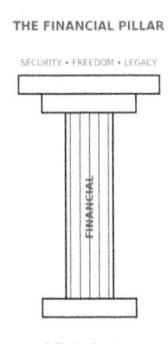

THE FINANCIAL PILLAR

SECURITY • FREEDOM • LEGACY

FINANCIAL

Reflection Questions:
1. What financial habits are serving your future legacy?
2. Where do you need more discipline or awareness with money?

CORNERSTONE TRUTHS

1. Money is a servant, not a master—it magnifies who you are.

2. Compound interest is underestimated but unstoppable when harnessed.
3. Financial mastery requires reframing beliefs, anchoring abundance, and daily discipline.

REFLECTION QUESTIONS

1. What beliefs about money did you inherit, and how can you reframe them?
2. How are you currently leveraging or neglecting the power of compounding?
3. What one financial discipline could you begin this week to align money with purpose?

"Wealth is not built in a day, but daily disciplines build wealth that lasts for generations."

PART THREE
INTEGRATION
AND EXPANSION

"Knowledge without application is useless. Application without reflection is shallow."

— ADAPTED FROM SOCRATES

By now, the structure of your life is visible, Cornerstones below, life areas above. But a blueprint isn't meant to stay on paper. It must be lived, tested, adjusted, and expanded. Part III is about integration: weaving together vocation, finances, influence, mindset, and spirit so that they no longer stand as isolated compartments, but as a unified whole. It's also about expansion: stretching what you believe is possible and discovering the leverage points that unlock exponential growth. This is where your life shifts from addition to multiplication.

CHAPTER TWELVE

INTEGRATION: WEAVING IT ALL TOGETHER

"If you know the Way broadly you will see it in everything."

— MIYAMOTO MUSASHI

IF YOU'VE EVER WALKED INTO A HOUSE WHERE THE WALLS stand but the rooms feel lifeless, you know what disintegration feels like. The structure is there, but the soul is missing. Many people live their lives the same way. They've mastered pieces of the puzzle, a career, some savings, maybe a relationship or two, but never put them together. The result is a life that looks solid from the outside but feels empty inside.

Integration is the turning point. It's the moment the blueprint becomes a living, breathing design. It's when your health is not just about exercise but about fueling the energy you need to play with your kids, lead with clarity, and live with joy. It's when your finances are not just about numbers, but about freedom, choices, and generosity. It's when your vocation is not just about work, but about service and purpose.

Integration is what turns categories into a symphony.

WHY INTEGRATION MATTERS

We've all been told to "balance" life, as if every area gets an equal slice of the pie. But life doesn't work that way. If you try to give everything equal attention, you'll end up exhausted and guilty, exhausted because you're spread too thin, guilty because no matter how much you do, something always feels neglected.

The truth is, life is not lived in silos. You don't get to pause your health while you focus on your business. You don't get to put your family on hold while you chase finances. Every decision you make touches multiple areas at once.

The way you spend your mornings, for example, ripples into everything. A rushed start filled with stress bleeds into your health, your mindset, and your relationships. But a deliberate start, exercise, reflection, and gratitude boost your energy, sharpen your mind, and steadies your presence for the people around you.

"Integration multiplies impact. One action, many returns."

This is why integration matters. Without it, life feels like juggling. With it, life feels like harmony.

THE INTEGRATION TRAP: DOING MORE ISN'T ALWAYS BETTER

Here's where most people who try to improve their lives get stuck. They read this super awesome, amazing, mind-blowing, revolutionary book about the seven life areas and immediately try to overhaul everything at once. They wake up determined to eat healthy, hit the gym, meditate, budget their finances, work on their marriage, focus more on their career, be more present with their kids, serve their community, and practice gratitude – all before lunch!

By Wednesday, they're exhausted. By Saturday, they've quit everything and have gone back to their old habits. Sound familiar, anyone?

And why? Because they misunderstood integration. They thought it meant doing more in every area, but they missed the secret that provides a shortcut – integration isn't addition, it's multiplication.

The secret isn't doing seven separate things. It's doing several things that touch multiple areas.

Let me give you an example: If you start running three mornings a week with your eldest son, you're not just working on your health. You're also strengthening your relationship (family). You're modeling discipline (mindset). You're teaching him that commitment matters

(Influence). Before you know it, those runs become sacred, where, immediately afterward, you have deep talks about life, faith, and purpose (spirit) while catching your breath in the garage.

Let me give you another one: A business owner who involves his teenage daughter in reviewing the company's financials isn't just working on his business, double-checking the numbers (vocation). He's teaching her financial literacy (finances). He's spending quality time with her (family), and she might even respect him more because of how successful he is. He's modeling stewardship and transparency (spirit). He's also preparing her to think as an owner one day (legacy / influence).

The mistake people make is thinking integration requires more time. It doesn't. it requires more intention. You're already spending time on things, you're just not being strategic about which things and how they're designed. Integration isn't about adding seven new practices to your day. It's about redesigning what you're already doing so each action creates compounding returns.

The wrong question: What else do I need to add?

The correct question: How can I design what I'm already doing to serve multiple areas at once?

That shift can change everything.

Reflection: Where in your life do you feel most "pulled

apart"? What would it look like if those areas supported each other instead of competing for your energy?

THE POWER OF ALIGNMENT

Think of integration less like balance and more like gears in a machine. Balance is static; gears are dynamic. When gears align, movement is smooth and powerful. When one gear slips, the whole machine grinds.

That's how life works. Health feeds vocation. Vocation feeds finances. Finances fuel family and relationships. Relationships strengthen spirit. Spirit fuels mindset. And mindset fuels everything.

When you integrate, these gears lock together. Suddenly, the effort you apply in one place drives momentum in every other place.

"The goal is not balance, it is alignment."

THE FOUR CORNERSTONES AS THREADS

Belief, Knowledge, Consistency, and Results are not just the foundation, they are the threads that weave through every life area.

- Belief sets the story: Do you believe health matters? Do you believe wealth can serve a purpose? Do you believe relationships are worth the work?

- Knowledge equips you: Financial literacy strengthens wealth and relieves stress that strains family. Communication skills deepen relationships and expand influence.
- Consistency is the rhythm: Showing up for a daily workout isn't just about fitness — it's a daily reminder that you can keep promises to yourself.
- Results are the proof: They show you the integration is working. Improved energy at work, deeper connection at home, more peace in spirit.

I used to think transformation required massive changes, big risks, big leaps, big breakthroughs. But what I've learned, both personally and watching others, is that sometimes the smallest habits create the biggest shifts.

For me, that habit was meditation. At first, it felt almost insignificant. Ten minutes in the morning, sitting quietly, slowing my breath, and learning to notice my thoughts instead of being run by them. But over time, it changed everything.

The first shift I noticed was in my mind. Stress that used to sit on my chest like a weight began to lift. Problems that once looked overwhelming suddenly felt workable. By calming my inner world, I had more clarity in my outer world.

That clarity spilled into my relationships. I became more present at home. My kids didn't just see a dad who was there, they saw a dad who was *with them*, not distracted or short-tempered. My wife noticed the difference too. When you learn to sit still in meditation, you also learn to listen deeper in conversation.

In business, meditation sharpened my leadership. Instead of reacting in the heat of the moment, I started responding with focus and intention. Decisions came with more patience, and my team felt steadier because I was steadier.

Even my physical health benefited. Stress eats at your body in ways you don't notice until it's too late. By lowering stress through meditation, I slept better, recovered faster, and had more energy to put into workouts and workdays alike.

One small cornerstone habit rippled into every area of my life. Meditation taught me that integration isn't about adding more plates to spin. It's about creating alignment, so that one simple act fuels every other dimension of who you are.

"Meditation isn't time wasted. It's energy invested."

PRACTICAL INTEGRATION

So how do you integrate? Start with keystone practices, habits that ripple outward.

- Morning Routine: Exercise (health), gratitude (spirit), reading (knowledge/mindset), and goal setting (vocation/finances). One routine, four areas elevated.
- Family Meals: Time together strengthens family bonds, improves health through home cooking, models stewardship for finances, and transmits values for influence.
- Purposeful Work: Aligning vocation with calling transforms daily effort into service (spirit), provision (finances), and self-respect (mindset).

Reflection: What one practice could you add this week that would impact at least three areas of your life at once?

THE COST OF FRAGMENTATION

What if you don't integrate? The price is steep. You become the business owner who builds wealth but loses health. The parent who provides but is absent. The achiever who wins influence but feels spiritually empty.

Fragmentation is costly. Integration is liberating.

"Fragmentation drains you. Integration frees you."

Now imagine the opposite: every action compounding. A workout not just shaping your body but fueling patience at home, focus at work, and resilience in spirit. A financial decision not just about money but about teaching stewardship to your children and aligning generosity with your values.

This is integration, compound interest applied to life.

WHAT IF YOU DESIGNED LIFE THIS WAY?

Picture your day:

- You wake up and move your body (health), while listening to an audiobook on leadership (vocation / knowledge), and finish with prayer or meditation (spirit).
- You eat breakfast with your family (relationships / family), sharing one insight you've gained (social influence).
- You work with clarity, knowing your vocation is aligned with purpose (vocation / spirit), and steward finances wisely (finances).
- You end your day with a walk with your partner (health / relationships), talking about shared goals (mindset).

That's not fantasy. That's design.

"Integration turns routines into rituals, and rituals into legacy."

Integration is the art of weaving. It's where the blueprint stops being lines on paper and becomes a life you actually live. It's where your Four Cornerstones thread through every Life Area until the whole tapestry is strong, resilient, and beautiful.

The next chapter will expand this principle into the world beyond you — influence. Because once your life is integrated, your impact multiplies. And when your impact multiplies, legacy begins.

CHAPTER THIRTEEN

BLUEPRINT: DESIGNING YOUR CORNERSTONE LIFE

"The best way to predict the future is to design it."

— PETER DRUCKER

EVERY GREAT STRUCTURE BEGINS WITH A BLUEPRINT. Architects don't improvise skyscrapers. Builders don't guess their way through foundations. Even the most modest family home begins with lines carefully drawn on paper. Without a blueprint, the result is chaos: walls where there should be doors, doors where there should be windows, and stress where there should be flow.

Your life deserves the same intention.

The Four Cornerstones and the Seven Life Areas are powerful by themselves, but without a design to unite them, they remain scattered. The blueprint is the moment where belief, knowledge, consistency, and results are mapped across health, family, relationships, vocation, finances, social influence, mindset, and spirit. It is where ideas turn into structure, and structure turns into destiny.

WHY DESIGN MATTERS

Before I get deep into this, I need to make an important distinction. I'm sharing how to create a blueprint, not a vision board. Nothing against vision-board-believing-people, but a blueprint has lines drawn, driven by data and experience; vision boards, to many, are wishful thinking.

A vision board would have a picture of six-pack abs, a million dollars, a perfect marriage, and their dream car, because, apparently, you can't have a vision board without the dream car. Oh, and they date they want all of it is the end of the next quarter.

A blueprint is derived from your current reality, and the most strategic step you can take in each life area. It then goes to building momentum from there.

Vision boards are aspirational. Blueprints are architectural. One feels inspiring in the moment, the other actually builds something over time.

I've watched countless people create elaborate life plans, usually at the beginning of every year. I've seen impressively detailed spreadsheets, ambitious goals, and motivational posters and quotes that make me feel as if I could run through a wall. But they've quit by February. The reason? Their plan wasn't rooted in reality. It was a fantasy dressed up as a blueprint.

A real blueprint accounts for constraints:

- Your current fitness level (not where you wish you were)
- Your actual income (not the income you hope to have someday. (I mean, why does someone who makes $60,000 a year have a Bugatti on their vision board?)
- Your real schedule (not the imaginary one where you have unlimited time and energy)
- Your existing commitments (family, work, responsibilities)
- Your genuine capacity (how much change can you actually sustain)

Here's the brutal truth: if your blueprint requires you to become a completely different person overnight, it's not a blueprint – it's a fictional story.

Real blueprints are built in phases. An architect doesn't design a skyscraper with the expectation that it be done in a week. There's excavation, foundation, framing, systems, finishing, etc. Each phase builds on the last.

Life works the same way. If you're currently working 60 hours a week, eating fast food, and haven't exercised in five years, your Year 1 blueprint doesn't need to include running the Boston Marathon and meditating two hours a day. That's fantasy.

A blueprint must be honest about where you are and realistic about where you can get to. It's not about lowering your standards – it's about raising your strategy. Start where you are. Build one solid layer at a time. Before you know it, you've constructed something that lasts. At one point, a little at a time becomes a lot.

Most people drift. They wake up, react to circumstances, and call it living. They wonder why progress is slow, why setbacks feel catastrophic, and why years slip by without the life they imagined taking shape. The reason is simple: they never designed it.

A blueprint does not guarantee perfection. It guarantees direction.

If you've ever remodeled a kitchen, you know how important this is. Without a plan, you overspend, move appliances twice, and argue about details you should have settled weeks before. But with a blueprint, you may still hit bumps in the road, a back-ordered cabinet, a late contractor, but the design keeps you anchored. You know what you're building.

That's what a life blueprint gives you. Anchoring. Direction. A plan that keeps you moving forward when circumstances shift.

Reflection: What would shift for you if you stopped drifting and started designing?

WHAT A LIFE BLUEPRINT LOOKS LIKE

A life blueprint is not a to-do list. It is not a rigid schedule or a punishing routine. It is a living design that captures the architecture of your values and priorities.

At its core, the blueprint answers four questions:

1. What do I believe is possible for me? (Belief)
2. What knowledge and tools do I need to build it? (Knowledge)
3. What consistent actions will make it real? (Consistency)
4. What feedback will confirm progress? (Results)

Now stretch those questions across the Seven Life Areas. Your health goals connect to your vocation goals. Your financial plans serve your family. Your mindset strengthens your spirit.

This is not compartmentalization — it is integration by design.

"If you don't design your life, someone else will design it for you."

THE ARCHITECTURE OF VALUES

Every blueprint is guided by values.

A builder's blueprint must meet codes, account for terrain, and serve the people who will live inside. Your life blueprint must account for what matters most.

Here's the secret: when your blueprint ignores your true values, you will sabotage it. You'll drag your feet, lose energy, and feel resentment. But when your blueprint reflects your values, energy flows.

For example:

- If family is your highest value, but your blueprint demands seventy-hour work weeks, you will resist it.
- If health is your highest value, but your blueprint ignores exercise and rest, you will eventually break down.
- If contribution is your highest value, but your blueprint focuses only on personal wealth, you will feel empty.

Reflection: List your top three values right now. Does your current life design reflect them, or fight them?

PRACTICAL TOOLS FOR DESIGNING YOUR LIFE

Here are three practical steps to put your blueprint on paper:

1. Vision Mapping
Draw your life ten years out in each of the Seven Life Areas. Be specific. How does your health feel? What does your family dynamic look like? What impact do you have socially? This is your destination.

2. Cornerstone Overlay

For each area, identify one belief to adopt, one piece of knowledge to pursue, one habit to practice consistently, and one result to measure. That gives you a framework rooted in the Four Cornerstones.

3. Integration Calendar

Instead of a rigid daily plan, design weekly rhythms that integrate multiple areas. For example, a Saturday morning hike with your family improves health, strengthens relationships, models consistency for your children, and connects spirit with nature.

"One rhythm aligned with your values is more powerful than a thousand scattered actions."

THE COST OF LIVING WITHOUT A BLUEPRINT

Imagine a builder trying to construct a house by memory. Each day they show up and decide on the spot what to do. A wall here, a pipe there. The result is predictable: wasted resources, endless rework, and collapse under pressure.

Now imagine living your life that way. Many people do. They pursue careers without clarity, relationships without intention, finances without stewardship, and health without discipline. The cost is staggering lost years, broken trust, financial strain, and spiritual emptiness.

Without a blueprint, you may achieve success in one area but sabotage another. You may win influence but lose health. Gain wealth but lose family. Reach goals but lose yourself.

Reflection: Where in your life have you been "building without a blueprint"?

THE HARD TRUTH: SOMETIMES PRIORITIES COMPETE

Here's something the self-help gurus don't share: even with a perfect blueprint, sometimes life areas crash into each other. Sometimes you can't give everything your all. Sometimes you have to choose which ones to work on and which to skip.

Real-life scenarios:

- You're in the middle of a critical business launch (vocation) right when your kid has a major school event (family).
- You're trying to get healthy and go to the gym (physical) but your aging parent needs care (family).
- You want to invest heavily in your business and attend a conference (finances/vocation), but

your marriage is struggling and needs more of your time (relationships)

What do you do when the blueprint says one thing, but reality demands another?

This is where values become your tiebreaker!

Remember your non-negotiables from earlier in the book? Those are your load-bearing walls. When priorities collide, you default to protecting those walls first – even if it costs you in other areas.

So even though you think you'd learn a lot at the conference, and even if you've already paid to go, if being present for your family is a non-negotiable, you miss the conference. You miss the meeting and attend the play. You miss the introduction and pick your son up from football practice.

WHAT IF YOU DESIGNED WITH CARE?

Now flip the vision. Imagine living with a blueprint that integrates everything.

- Your morning begins with habits that strengthen health, mindset, and spirit.
- Your vocation aligns with values, providing finances and purpose.
- Your family rhythms build bonds while modeling consistency for your children.

- Your influence grows naturally because people trust a life that is congruent.

This is not theory. It is the compound effect of design. One choice, multiplied by time, creates legacy.

"Blueprints don't just build houses. They build futures."

In the early years of my business, everything was chaos. Phones ringing off the hook, jobs double-booked, paperwork stacked so high it looked like it might topple. Most days, it felt like I was sprinting just to stay one step ahead of disaster. I told myself this was the price of entrepreneurship: long hours, endless stress, constant firefighting. But deep down, I knew the truth: I was running on grit, not design.

One night, after another 14-hour day that left me staring at the ceiling at 2 a.m., it hit me: if I didn't build a system, the business would eventually break me. Hustle wasn't sustainable. Chaos was robbing me of peace, my family of my presence, and my team of stability.

That realization became the turning point. I sat down with a blank notebook and asked myself, what would this look like if it were simple? Out of that question came the first blueprint. We mapped how calls came in, how jobs were scheduled, how pricing was standardized, how the money flowed. Every piece that had once lived in my head or in scattered scraps of paper started to take form on the page.

The effect was immediate. Instead of drowning in noise, I had clarity. The team suddenly had something to follow that wasn't just "ask Steve." Customers felt the difference too, jobs were smoother, communication clearer, and service more consistent.

But the biggest shift wasn't just in the business. It was in me. Structure brought peace. For the first time, I felt momentum building that didn't depend solely on me grinding harder. The blueprint gave me something I could trust, and because of that, I could finally breathe.

That experience taught me a truth I'll never forget design beats hustle. Hustle might get you started, but only a blueprint gets you free.

"Chaos isn't the price of growth. Clarity is the blueprint for freedom."

The breakthrough of building systems in my business was so powerful that I eventually asked myself: What if I applied the same principle to my life?

At that point, my personal world often mirrored the business chaos. Days blurred into nights. Family time got squeezed between phone calls. Health and self-care were "if there's time" items, and there was never time. I was showing up everywhere but never fully present anywhere.

So I took the same notebook I had once used to map the business and began drawing a blueprint for my life. I asked: What matters most to me? What are the non-negotiables? Where does my energy actually need to go?

From those questions came structure. Family dinners got scheduled like board meetings. Workouts went into the calendar as appointments I couldn't skip. Morning routines became rituals of alignment, mind, body, and spirit, before I let the world in. I even carved out sacred time with my wife and kids, treating those moments as the highest-return investments I could ever make.

The results were dramatic. My stress didn't just drop, my presence skyrocketed. The same way customers noticed the difference when my business had systems, my family noticed the difference when my life had a blueprint. I wasn't scattered anymore. I was grounded.

That experience taught me that freedom doesn't come from having more time. Freedom comes from clarity about how you use the time you already have. And just like in business, the blueprint wasn't about restriction — it was about alignment.

"Blueprints don't box you in. They set you free."

The blueprint is not meant to sit in a drawer. It must be tested, adapted, and lived. The next step is to take the design and implement it consistently. Because once you commit to living your design, you stop being a dreamer and become a legacy builder.

CHAPTER FOURTEEN

LEGACY: LIVING BEYOND YOURSELF

"Carve your name on hearts, not tombstones. A legacy is etched into the minds of others and the stories they share about you."

— SHANNON L. ALDER

MOST PEOPLE THINK LEGACY IS ABOUT WHAT YOU LEAVE behind when you die. That's part of it, but it's not the whole truth. Legacy isn't just about the money, the property, or even the name etched on a building. True legacy is about the ripple effect of your life while you are still alive. It's about how your beliefs, actions, and character echo through the lives of others long before your final chapter is written.

Legacy is not a someday concept. It's a today practice. Every conversation, every decision, every consistent act of integrity becomes a thread in the story others will remember.

WHY LEGACY MATTERS

Here's the truth: everyone leaves a legacy, whether they intend to or not. Some leave a legacy of bitterness, broken trust, and squandered opportunities. Others leave a legacy of resilience, wisdom, and love. The question isn't whether you will leave one. The question is: what kind will it be?

Whether you think about legacy or not, your life will answer three questions for everyone who knows you. The questions don't change; you have no control over them. What you have control over is what the answers will be.

QUESTION 1: DID THEY KEEP THEIR WORD?

Were they trustworthy? Integrity is the foundation of every lasting legacy. When people think of you, will they remember someone whose word was their bond? Or will they remember you as someone with a big heart who promised much but delivered little?

This isn't about perfectionism or finances – it's about character. Did you show up when you said you would? Did you donate what you said you would? Did you follow through even when it was hard? Did you do what you said, even when no one was watching? Are people going to say that regardless of the time or place, if you said you would be there, they knew you would be there?

Will your children, who you are more of yourself than even with your spouse, say your yes meant yes and your no meant no? Will your employees say you held yourself to the same standards you asked them to? Will your spouse say the person you promised to be on your wedding day is the person you became?

Integrity may not get headlines, but it builds legacies that last for generations.

QUESTION 2: DID THEY MAKE OTHERS BETTER?

It's not about accumulation, it's measured by what you cultivated in others. Did you develop people, or did you use them? Did you invest in growth or just extract productivity? Did you leave people stronger, wiser, and more capable than how you found them?

The true test of leadership isn't what happens when you're in the room, it's what happens when you leave the building. I hate to break it to you, but if everything falls apart without you, you're not building a legacy, you're nurturing dependency.

But if people thrive because of what you taught them, equipped them, and modeled for them, that's legacy. That's multiplication and impact that outlives you.

QUESTION 3: DID THEY LIVE WHAT THEY BELIEVED?

The most powerful legacy is congruence; alignment between what you said and how you lived. Some people preach about health as they destroy their bodies. Some talk about the importance of family while neglecting their own. As the owner, you can demand integrity and doing the job right the first time, yet still cut corners. It doesn't matter what you preach if you don't live it, because before people will do what you say, they'll do what you do.

Congruence is the difference between a legacy of inspiration and a legacy of hypocrisy. When your life aligns with your words, you give people someone they can trust. Someone they can model.

These three questions: integrity, investment in others, and congruence, are the scorecard of legacy.

If you live only for yourself, your impact ends with you. But when you live for others, when you allow your Four Cornerstones to shape not just your life but the lives you touch, your influence multiplies. Your children inherit your habits. Your team absorbs your mindset. Your community reflects your values.

"Legacy is less about what you leave and more about who you become."

THE BLUEPRINT OF LEGACY

Legacy rests on the same foundation as everything we've discussed: belief, knowledge, consistency, and results. But now the blueprint extends beyond your personal life into others' lives.

- Belief: Do you believe your life matters enough to influence others? Do you believe your story is worth passing on?
- Knowledge: What wisdom, principles, and skills can you intentionally transfer to others?
- Consistency: Are you living in a way that others can reliably follow? Do your words match your actions?
- Results: What outcomes prove that your life has shaped others for the better?

Legacy is not built by grand gestures alone. It's built by the thousand invisible ways you show up consistently, especially when no one is watching.

If your children, employees, or friends lived exactly as you live, would you be proud of the legacy they inherited?

THE MYTH OF SOMEDAY

Too many people postpone legacy. They tell themselves: Once I hit my financial goals, then I'll give back. Once the kids are grown, then I'll mentor. Once I retire, then I'll think about legacy.

But here's the truth: legacy is built in the ordinary. It's built in the dinner conversations, the decisions under pressure, the way you treat people who can't offer you anything in return.

You don't intentionally build legacy; you live your life, and the legacy is a byproduct.

"Legacy is not tomorrow's gift — it is today's practice."

PRACTICAL FRAMEWORKS FOR LEGACY

So how do you design legacy with intention? Here are three pathways:

1. Personal Legacy
This is the impact you leave within your family and closest relationships. Are you teaching your children resilience? Are you modeling consistency in your marriage? Are you passing on stories of faith, courage, and growth?

2. Professional Legacy
This is the impact you leave on the people you lead, serve, or mentor. Are you developing people, or merely using them for results? Are you

building systems others can thrive in or are you leaving behind chaos?

3. Social Legacy

This is the impact you leave on your community and society. Are you giving time, wisdom, or resources? Are you leaving behind neighborhoods, businesses, and communities stronger than you found them?

"Your greatest legacy is not in what you build, but in who you build."

When people talk about legacy, they often point to wealth, fame, or accomplishments carved in stone. But when I think about legacy, I think of something quieter, something deeper, the kind of impact that isn't measured in headlines but in habits, not in applause but in character.

For me, that legacy begins with my dad.

As a kid, I didn't see it that way. At six years old, being dragged out of bed before sunrise to deliver newspapers every morning didn't feel like a gift. It felt like punishment. On Sundays, it was even worse, hundreds of papers stacked high in the Bronco, the weight of responsibility heavier than I thought I could carry. While my friends had sleepovers and lazy mornings, I had routes to finish. At that age, I couldn't understand why a father who "loved" me would make me do that. So, I built a belief that maybe he didn't like me.

That belief stuck for years. It colored the way I saw him and, in some ways, the way I saw myself. I mistook discipline for distance, responsibility for rejection.

But life has a way of revealing truth at the right time. In my twenties, I sat in a training room and heard someone say, *"Everyone is doing the best they can with what they have."* Those words broke something open in me. Suddenly, I saw my dad differently. He wasn't trying to hurt me. He was preparing me.

Every early morning paper route was a lesson in consistency. Every demand for discipline was training for endurance. Every refusal to let me quit was his way of teaching me to carry weight, not just newspapers, but the weight of life. My dad may not have had the language to tell me he believed in me, but he had the conviction to shape me into a man who could stand.

Now, as a father myself, I see his legacy in sharper focus. It shows up every time I push through when others would quit. It shows up when I choose responsibility over excuses. It shows up when I tell my kids, not just with words but with my example, that love isn't always soft, sometimes it's strong, steady, and demanding, because the world demands even more.

My dad didn't leave behind fame or fortune. He left behind something greater: a legacy of consistency, work ethic, and resilience that lives in me, and through me, in my family and everyone I interact with.

One day, my children will tell their own stories about me. My hope is that they won't just remember what I built, but how I lived. That they'll feel the echo of my dad's lessons, passed down through me to them. That they'll understand what I finally came to see: the quiet, often misunderstood ways a father loves his child are sometimes the loudest legacy of all.

"Legacy isn't about what you leave for your children. It's about what you leave in them."

Legacy lives in:

- The way you talk to your spouse when you're tired and irritated
- Whether you keep your word when its inconvenient
- How you respond when your kid interrupts you during work
- If you pray before meals when no one is watching
- Whether you tell the truth when a lie would be easier
- How you treat the waitress, gas station attendant, and strangers

- If you show up to the game, the recital, and the mundane Tuesday dinners

These moments feel nearly insignificant. But, over the years, they built a pattern. And that pattern becomes your legacy.

COMPOUND INTEREST OF LEGACY

Legacy works like compound interest. At first, the returns seem small: a conversation here, a habit modeled there. But over the years, the impact multiplies.

Think about it: a single sentence of encouragement can shape the trajectory of someone's career. A consistent morning ritual can inspire a child to value discipline. A pattern of generosity can ripple through generations.

The reason many people underestimate legacy is that they underestimate the small, consistent things. They believe legacy is about big speeches and headlines, but it's about the little daily deposits that add up to a fortune of influence.

Ask yourself, what small habit or action could you commit to that, multiplied over decades, would transform the people closest to you?

LIVING BEYOND YOURSELF

Legacy is about moving from success to significance. Success is about what you achieve. Significance is about what others achieve because of you.

- Success is building wealth.
- Significance is teaching your children stewardship.
- Success is climbing the ladder.
- Significance is sending the elevator back down.
- Success is achieving freedom.
- Significance is using that freedom to free others.
- "Success is what you gain. Legacy is what you give."

IN CLOSING

When the blueprint of your life is aligned, integration flows naturally into legacy. What you design for yourself becomes a gift to others. What you practice in private becomes inspiration in public.

Legacy isn't about waiting until the end. It's about living every day as if someone else's future depends on it, because it does.

The next step is stepping into Part IV: Application and Expansion, where we'll bring everything together in practical strategies for living your Cornerstone Life every day.

PART FOUR
LIVING THE BLUEPRINT

"There's no crying in plumbing."

— STEVEN J. ADDARIO SR.

The final part of this volume is not an ending, but a beginning. Here, you'll take the blueprint off the page and into your daily reality. Living the Blueprint means embodying it in your choices, your habits, your relationships, and your vision for the future. It is where wisdom becomes action, and action becomes legacy. By the time you reach the conclusion, you will not simply understand the Four Cornerstones or the Seven Life Areas, you will be living them. And when you live them, life itself transforms.

CONCLUSION – LIVING THE CORNERSTONE BLUEPRINT

"The unexamined life is not worth living."

— SOCRATES

We have traveled through the Four Cornerstones and explored how they support the Seven Life Areas. Along the way, we have seen that success, fulfillment, and legacy are not accidents, they are built on foundations. Your beliefs, knowledge, consistency, and results form the structure, while health, family, relationships, vocation, finances, social influence, mindset, and spirit become the rooms of your life's house. When aligned, they create wholeness. When misaligned, life feels fractured.

The journey of this book has been about integration. Too often, we separate life into compartments, work, health, and relationships, without realizing they are connected. Neglect one area, and the others weaken. Strengthen one, and the others grow stronger. This is the wisdom of The Cornerstone Blueprint.

Think of your life as a building. The Four Cornerstones form the foundation. Belief sets the vision, Knowledge lays the foundation, Consistency builds day to day, and Results prove the structure is sound. On this foundation stand the Seven Life Areas, the walls, roof, and interior. Without the foundation, the house collapses. Without the walls, the foundation remains unused. Together, they form a complete dwelling.

Or think of life as a compass. Each cornerstone is a directional point, and the Seven Life Areas are the terrain you navigate. Without the compass, you are lost. Without the terrain, the compass has no journey to guide. Together, they create progress.

Why does this matter? Because without an integrated framework, most people drift. They chase health at the expense of family. They build finances but neglect spirit. They succeed in vocation but collapse in relationships. Without balance, there is no peace. With balance, life becomes coherent, meaningful, and impactful.

The Cornerstone Blueprint does not promise ease. It promises alignment. Alignment means living true to your values, growing daily, and serving beyond your-self. That is the essence of fulfillment.

History's greatest figures lived with such alignment. Nelson Mandela aligned spirit with vocation and social influence. Mother Teresa aligned spirit with service and family beyond blood. Entrepreneurs like Elon Musk align their vocation with their mindset and social impact. Every life of greatness reveals the same truth: the blueprint works across time and culture.

Greatness is not reserved for icons. Consider a father who balances his vocation with presence at home, raising children rooted in love and confidence. Or a nurse who integrates spirit, vocation, and compassion into every patient interaction. These lives rarely make headlines, but they quietly shape the world. The blueprint is as much about ordinary greatness as it is about extraordinary achievement.

What if you ignored these principles? Imagine a life of scattered effort—beliefs unexamined, knowledge shallow, consistency broken. Health fails, relationships fracture, finances fluctuate, and spirit dries up. At the end, you wonder, 'What was it all for?'

Now imagine living the blueprint. Belief strong, knowledge expanding, consistency steady, results multiplying. Health vibrant, family connected, vocation purposeful, finances abundant, relationships rich, spirit alive. At the end, you rest in peace knowing you lived fully, loved deeply, and served greatly.

Project this 30 years forward. Without alignment, stress and regret compound. With alignment, growth and peace compound. Like compound interest in finances, the small daily deposits of the blueprint accumulate into exponential dividends of joy, meaning, and legacy.

Here is a final NLP-inspired integration exercise:

1. Close your eyes and imagine standing in the center of a house. The foundation beneath you is strong—the Four Cornerstones.
2. Around you are seven rooms—each representing a life area. See each one filled with light, order, and abundance.
3. Anchor this image with a gesture or phrase (e.g., placing your hand on your heart and saying, 'Aligned').
4. Walk mentally through each room—see yourself thriving in health, connecting with family, building vocation, managing finances, and deepening your spirit.
5. Visualize living each day in this house—stable, whole, and vibrant.
6. Future pace: see yourself decades from now, surrounded by the fruits of alignment—health, love, wealth, peace, and legacy.
7. Write down your vision. Language crystallizes thought and thought directs destiny.

The first time I realized the power of belief, it didn't come through success. It came through struggle. Growing up, I carried the thought that my dad didn't like me, that no matter what I did, I wasn't enough. That belief shaped the way I saw myself, until one day, I heard someone say, *"Everyone is doing the best they can with what they have."*

That one truth dismantled years of misunderstanding. It reframed my entire childhood. My dad's discipline wasn't rejection; it was preparation. That shift in belief became a cornerstone. From then on, I understood: if you want to change your life, you don't just change your circumstances, you change your beliefs.

That discovery has impacted every part of my life since. Belief is no longer a hidden thermostat keeping me cold when I want warmth. It's a lever I can raise higher, knowing my results will rise with it.

"Change your belief, and you change your destiny."

But legacy isn't built on wins alone. Some of the most powerful lessons came from neglect.

There was a season when I ignored my family in the name of growing the business. I told myself I was doing it for them, but the truth was I was doing it for me, for pride, for ambition, for numbers on a page. The cost was real. Missed dinners. Missed games. The look in my kids' eyes when they asked if I'd be home, and I didn't have an answer.

That neglect shaped me. It taught me that success in one area can't compensate for emptiness in another. No amount of revenue erases regret. And no trophy fills the space left by absence at home.

The pain of that season became the blueprint for change. I shifted my priorities, realigned the business around my family instead of away from them, and committed to never sacrificing the most important people for the sake of achievement.

"If one pillar crumbles, the whole house feels it."

The Cornerstone Blueprint isn't theory. It's lived. It's built in beliefs reshaped, knowledge applied, consistency endured, and results earned. It's tested in physical discipline, mental strength, spiritual grounding, familial love, social bonds, vocational calling, and financial wisdom.

Living this blueprint doesn't mean life will be easy. It means life will be aligned. And alignment is where power lives.

This is your invitation. Raise your belief thermostat. Sharpen your knowledge. Commit to consistency. Demand results. Build your blueprint. Live your legacy.

Because at the end of it all, the question won't be how much you built, but who you became.

"Legacy is the echo of your alignment. Live it well."

Picture yourself one year from today. You have applied the blueprint. Your mornings begin with clarity. Your days feel purposeful. Your relationships thrive. Challenges come, but you respond with resilience. People notice your presence—steady, grounded, and inspiring.

Picture yourself ten years from today. The compounding of alignment has multiplied. You are healthier than your peers, closer with your family, more fulfilled in work, freer financially, richer in spirit. You have become a lighthouse for others. Your life itself is a message.

Picture yourself thirty years from today. The generations that follow you live stronger because of the foundation you laid. Your children carry forward your values. Your community thrives because of your influence. Your spirit continues to ripple through lives you may never meet. This is legacy... the true measure of a life well lived.

This book has focused on life. But the blueprint does not stop here. Just as it transforms health, family, relationships, and spirit, it also transforms business. Volume 2 will explore how these same principles create enterprises that thrive—businesses built not just for profit but for legacy. It will show how to align teams, scale revenue, and build empires without losing balance. Life and business are not separate; they are two arenas of the same soul.

Your personal life is the laboratory. Business becomes the stage. Volume 2 will take the lessons of this book and apply them to leadership, culture, sales, and wealth. It will equip you to build enterprises that serve people, create freedom, and endure for generations. The Four Cornerstones do not change; they expand their reach.

Remember: you are both architect and builder. The materials of your life are already in your hands. What matters now is the design you choose and the effort you invest. The Cornerstone Blueprint is your design. The rest is choice, discipline, and faith.

CORNERSTONE TRUTHS

1. The Four Cornerstones provide the foundation for every life area.
2. Neglect one area, and the structure weakens. Strengthen one, and all grow stronger.
3. Integration, not isolation, is the key to fulfillment.

REFLECTION QUESTIONS

1. Which of the Four Cornerstones needs the most attention in your life right now?
2. Which of the Seven Life Areas feels most aligned? Which feels weakest?
3. What one action will you take this week to strengthen the blueprint in your daily life?
4. What is the legacy you want your life to leave, and how can you begin building it now?

"You are the architect of your destiny. Lay the foundation well, and the structure of your life will stand for generations."

ONE FINAL ACKNOWLEDGMENT

To my brother Joe, from the very first day of this ride, you've been beside me. We've walked through storms, fought battles, and carried burdens few will ever understand. When others drifted, you stayed. When the road grew dark, you didn't flinch. Through it all, you've been more than a brother, you've been my shield, my ally, my constant.

Every warrior needs someone they can trust with their back. You've been that for me, through every chapter, every trial, every victory, and every season of this journey thus far.

My journey hasn't been easy, but knowing you were in it with me gave me the strength to keep pushing forward. From the beginning to the end, through blood, sweat, and sacrifice, we've stood together.

And that, brother, is a legacy all its own.

ABOUT THE AUTHOR

Steven J. Addario Jr. is the founder of Addario's Services, a family-operated home service company based in Massachusetts. What began as a small plumbing and heating business has grown under his leadership into a multi-trade organization serving tens of thousands of households, delivering plumbing, HVAC, electrical, and remodeling solutions across the region.

With nearly three decades of experience in the home service industry, Steven has led his company through the challenges of growth, competition, and change, scaling sales into the tens of millions while maintaining the values of family, service, and integrity. His philosophy blends practical business strategy with personal development, and it is this integration that gave rise to Trades Talk, the coaching and consulting platform he founded to serve other business owners.

Trades Talk is more than a business, it is a movement designed to help service entrepreneurs break free from struggle, align with their highest values, and build the companies and lives they've always dreamed of. Through events, workshops, and mentorship, Steven equips leaders with the Four Cornerstones framework and applies it to every area of life and business.

Beyond the boardroom, Steven is husband to his high school sweetheart, Alison, and a father to four children. His deepest values are to grow himself, grow others, and build generational wealth. He believes true success is measured not only in revenue but in relationships, impact, and legacy.

This book, *The Cornerstone Blueprint*, is the first in a series designed to guide readers through aligning the Four Cornerstones with both life and business. Volume One focuses on life mastery; Volume Two will focus on business mastery. Together, they form a complete path for those who want to live fully, lead boldly, and leave behind a legacy that endures.

To learn more about Steven's work, upcoming events, and resources, visit TradesTalk.com. Join the Trades Talk movement and step into your own blueprint for life and business. Scan the QR code below.

INVITATION TO THE
JOURNEY AHEAD

If you are reading these words, it means you have walked with me through the Four Cornerstones and the Seven Life Areas. You've invested your time and your heart in exploring what it means to build a life of alignment, balance, and purpose. For that, I want to say thank you, not as an author to a reader, but as a fellow traveler to another. You have chosen growth, and that choice alone sets you apart.

But reading is only the beginning. Transformation does not happen from words on a page; it happens when ideas become action. The real work begins now, in the choices you make today, tomorrow, and the weeks that follow. My invitation is simple: take the Four Cornerstones and begin applying them in your own life. Reflect on your beliefs. Expand your knowledge. Commit to consistency. Measure your results. Do this daily, and you will see shifts that ripple outward through every area of your life.

And remember you are not alone in this work. Trades Talk was born to be a community for leaders, dreamers, and builders like you, men and women who want more than survival, who want mastery. Whether you're an entrepreneur, a professional, or someone simply hungry to grow, you are welcome here. Through workshops, coaching, and collaboration, we walk this path together. Growth multiplies when it's shared.

This book marks the end of Volume One, but it is also the beginning of what comes next. In Volume Two, we will turn the same blueprint toward business. If Volume One was about building the house of your personal life, Volume Two will be about building the empire of your professional life. We will explore how the Four Corner-stones create sustainable companies, scalable teams, and cultures that endure. You will see how alignment in business is not just about revenue, but about freedom, impact, and generational wealth.

I want you to see this book not as a conclusion, but as a springboard. The habits you build here will prepare you for the journey ahead. As you live the blueprint in your personal life, you are laying the groundwork for leader-ship in business, in community, and in legacy.

So here is my challenge: don't let this book sit on a shelf. Don't let the insights fade into memory. Choose one cornerstone to strengthen this week. Choose one life area to bring into alignment. Take one small, deliberate action. Write it down. Share it with someone. Anchor it into your routine. These small, consistent choices will compound, just like wealth, into extraordinary transformation.

If these pages stirred something in you and you are a business owner then I invite you deeper. Join the movement. Come into the Trades Talk community. Learn, grow, and walk alongside others who refuse to settle for mediocrity. Visit TradesTalk.com to connect with resources, events, and coaching opportunities that can accelerate your journey. Don't do this alone, because none of us were meant to.

The next step is yours. You've held the blueprint in your hands. Now build with it. My hope is that years from now, you will look back on this moment as the turning point, the day you decided not just to live, but to live fully. And when that day comes, I hope you will have built a life so rich, so aligned, and so impactful that generations after you will still feel its foundation.

"The blueprint is in your hands. The future is in your choices. Now act."

— Steven J. Addario Jr

INVITATION TO THE JOURNEY AHEAD